POWER STANDARDS

Identifying the Standards that Matter the Most

LARRY AINSWORTH, M.S.

Foreword by Douglas B. Reeves, Ph.D.

ISBN #0-9709455-4-X

Advanced Learning Press books are available for quantity discounts with bulk purchases for education systems, professional organizations, or sales promotion use. For more details and discount information, contact Advanced Learning Press at (800) 844-6599 or fax (303) 504-9417.

Editor: Allison Wedell Schumacher

Printed and Bound in the United States of America

Published by:
Advanced Learning Press
317 Inverness Way South, Suite 150, Englewood, CO 80112
(800) 844-6599 or (303) 504-9312 • Fax (303) 504-9417
www.makingstandardswork.com

Distributed by:
Center for Performance Assessment

Library of Congress Cataloging-in-Publication Data

Ainsworth, Larry.
    Power standards : identifying the standards that matter the most / Larry Ainsworth ;
  foreword by Douglas B. Reeves.
      p. cm.
  Includes bibliographical references and index.
    ISBN 0-9709455-4-X (pbk.)
    1. Education--Standards--United States. I. Title

LB3060.83.A38 2003
379.1'58'0973--dc21

Dedication

I respectfully dedicate this book to Douglas B. Reeves, founder and chairman of the Center for Performance Assessment. Dr. Reeves pioneered the concept of Power Standards and established a practical process any school system can use to identify its own Power Standards. His insights and guidance have significantly enhanced my own Power Standards presentations to school systems all over the country. I am deeply grateful for the profound influence he has had on me, on my colleagues at the Center, and on the thousands of educators with whom I have had the good fortune to share these ideas. Without the theoretical and practical insights he has so generously shared, this book would not have been possible.

About the Author

Larry Ainsworth is the Executive Director of Professional Development at the Center for Performance Assessment in Denver, Colorado. He travels widely throughout the United States to assist school systems in implementing standards and standards-based performance assessments in the K-12 classroom. He also leads seminars in Data-Driven Decision Making as well as workshops based on the two books he co-authored with Jan Christinson, *Student Generated Rubrics: An Assessment Model to Help All Students Succeed,* and *Five Easy Steps to a Balanced Math Program.* Larry's primary motivation is to assist educators in helping all students succeed by "taking the mystery out" of the instruction, learning, and assessment process.

Larry has delivered keynote addresses nationwide, most notably for the U.S. Department of Education, New York Department of Education, Ohio Department of Education, Michigan Department of Education, Harvard University Graduate School of Education's Principals' Center, Indiana Association for Supervision and Curriculum Development (ASCD), California ASCD, Virginia Title I and STARS conferences, and the Southern Regional Education Board. He has conducted breakout sessions at national and regional conferences throughout the country, including the California Math Council, the California International Studies Project, the Alabama CLAS Summer Institute, the Delaware Professional Development Conference, the National Council of Teachers of Mathematics, the National ASCD conference, and the National School Conference Institute.

With 24 years of experience as an upper-elementary and middle school classroom educator in demographically diverse schools, Larry brings a varied background and wide range of professional experiences to each of his presentations. He has held numerous leadership roles within school districts, including mentor teacher and K-12 math committee co-chair, and has served as a mathematics assessment consultant in several San Diego County school districts.

In addition to continuing his full-time presentation schedule, Larry has authored two newly published books, *Power Standards* and *"Unwrapping" The Standards.*

Larry holds a Master of Science degree in educational administration.

Acknowledgments

There are so many to thank for their contributions to this published work. First, I wish to express my appreciation to my Center for Performance Assessment colleagues, most notably Dr. Douglas Reeves, Eileen Allison, and Nan Woodson, as well as Janelle Miller, Ken Bingenheimer, Angie Hodapp, and Anne Fenske. Special thanks to my editor, Allison Wedell Schumacher, for preparing this book and its companion volume, *"Unwrapping" The Standards*, for publication with the same level of conscientiousness she demonstrated with my second book, *Five Easy Steps to a Balanced Math Program*, co-authored with Jan Christinson.

Secondly, I would like to thank the individuals and school systems that have so generously shared for this book their Power Standards process, examples of their identified Power Standards, and their success stories that have come as a result of implementing these ideas. Foremost among these are Dr. Karen Gould, Carole Erlandson, Michele Walker, Dr. Janet Boyle, and Paul Buck of Wayne Township, Indianapolis, Indiana; Rick Miller and Margo Healy of Caldwell School District, Caldwell, Idaho; Frank Tinney and Lorraine Becker of Palm Springs Unified School District, Palm Springs, California; Jim Fuller of Newark Unified School District, Newark, California; Jim Armstrong of the Santa Maria Joint Union High School District, Santa Maria, California; Ed Mathes of the Montgomery County, Ohio, Educational Service Center; Susan E. Riegle, principal, Mark Jones, educator, and the faculty of New Lebanon Middle School, New Lebanon, Ohio.

Lastly, to *all* the educators and administrators across the country with whom I have worked to identify Power Standards in their own schools and districts, I extend my most sincere thanks and appreciation for your receptivity to these ideas, your insightful comments and questions, and your conscientious application of these practices.

Contents

Detailed Contents

Chapter 3

Chapter 4

Foreword

"I just don't have the time!" This is the most common complaint I hear from educators and school leaders. If you or your colleagues have ever felt overwhelmed by the demands of too many standards and too much curriculum in too few classroom hours, then this book is the answer you have been seeking. In the past decade, textbooks have grown heavier and curricula more dense as publishers, state departments of education, and central office administrators have in too many cases produced documents and policies that substituted girth for analysis. The typical response to this dilemma has been a series of rancorous diatribes against standards, as if the elimination of academic standards and a retreat to the "good old days" would solve our problems. In the following pages, you find not rancor but reason. You will not find destructive whining but constructive step-by-step solutions to the number one question vexing schools across the nation: How can we meet the complex learning needs of students in a standards-based environment? In brief, how can we achieve standards without becoming standardized?

No one is more qualified to address these challenges than Larry Ainsworth. A veteran classroom educator and popular speaker and author, Larry's present responsibilities as Executive Director of Professional Development with the Center for Performance Assessment bring him into contact with a broad range of teachers, administrators, students, parents, and policymakers. He provides sound theories substantiated by real-world case studies and examples of dramatic improvements in student achievement. When Larry Ainsworth talks about standards, people listen. Typical are comments such as, "I've heard dozens of speeches about standards and it was always abstract—just one more thing for me to do. Finally, it makes sense. I not only know what to do, but I understand why we are doing it." In these pages, Larry brings the same insight, humor, gentility, respect, and rigor that he provides to every professional development seminar he leads. Whether he is providing keynote addresses to national audiences, workshops to a dozen teachers in a rural area, or a seminar for hundreds of leaders and policymakers in a challenging urban setting, Larry's fundamental message does not change: Standards are fair. Standards are effective. And they will never be implemented solely by virtue of a state mandate. Their effective implementation will be the result of professionals collaborating at the local level to prioritize and apply the standards in a practical classroom setting.

Great teachers sometimes do their best work unconsciously. Their mastery of their subject allows them to achieve deep insight without announcing, "Warning! Deep insight follows!" There are, however, two deep insights in this book that are not announced with clarion calls but which are nevertheless vital for the reader to notice and understand. First, the author has resolved the "standards paradox" in which there are simultaneously too many and too few standards. It is clear to most teachers who lack a 400-day school year and pupils with photographic memories, that there are simply too many standards. Yet at the same time, there are too few standards, particularly if we note the paucity of standards regarding fairness, ethical behavior, appropriate citation of works created by others, time management, teamwork, and what, in a bygone era, we called "deportment." The notion of Power Standards resolves this paradox by narrowing the focus of academic requirements while at the same time recognizing that every teacher has to emphasize other knowledge and skills that may not be specified in state standards documents.

The second insight, perhaps even more important, that the author provides is the inherent connection between standards and assessment. An analogy can be drawn between standards documents in their present form and what the cynic said about marriage—namely, that hope triumphs over experience. This infantile fantasy suggests that by merely wishing to make something happen, it will be so. With experience, however, comes the realization that there is a gulf between desire and reality. In the context of standards, the mere articulation of student expectations is the academic equivalent of the infantile fantasy. *Without* the link to assessment, not one-shot state tests, but to the daily practice of classroom assessment, along with feedback, encouragement, coaching, and more than a little love added to the mixture, standards are little more than colorful wall charts. *With* the link to assessment and teaching practice as advocated in the following pages, standards will leap off the wall charts and into the daily lives of educators and students.

— *Dr. Douglas B. Reeves*

Dr. Reeves is the Chairman of the Center for Performance Assessment. He is the author of 14 books and serves on the faculty of the Harvard Leadership and Policy Forum. Dr. Reeves is also the recipient of the 2003 Harvard Distinguished Authors Award for *Daily Disciplines of Leadership*.

Introduction

So many standards, so little time! How can educators at every grade level and in every content area effectively teach and assess all the standards within the given instructional time each year?

Standards—unlike so many passing trends in education—are here to stay. All 50 states (Iowa has determined standards at the local level) and Washington, D.C., have formally established academic content standards that specify what students are expected to know and be able to do at each grade level in the various content areas. The federal reauthorization of the Elementary and Secondary Education Act of 2001—"No Child Left Behind"—now requires that *all* students demonstrate proficiency in reading and math as measured on state assessments by the end of the 2013-14 school year. States are to begin testing students in reading and math by the end of the 2005-06 school year. Schools will have to meet their AYP ("adequate yearly progress") performance targets, not only for the student population as a whole but also for various subgroups: students from racial and ethnic minorities, students with disabilities, students who are economically disadvantaged, and those with limited English proficiency (2002). This requirement is placing enormous accountability pressure on everyone involved. Because these high-stakes assessments are to be aligned with state standards, the standards have naturally become the critical focus for achieving the results that schools are expected to produce. To meet these rigorous demands, our educators need practical strategies, not only to realize higher student achievement levels in reading and mathematics, but also in every other content area.

Standards have the potential to significantly sharpen and focus curriculum, instruction, and assessment. However, educators and administrators are acutely aware of the fact that most state standards are too voluminous to be taught effectively within the number of instructional days each year. In striving to "cover" everything, many educators admit to teaching many of the standards only superficially. Often all standards are considered equal when, in fact, certain standards are more important than others in terms of overall student success. There is uncertainty and inconsistency regarding which standards educators need to emphasize over others. As a result, the use of standards to focus instruction and thus improve student learning is diminished.

What *Are* Power Standards?

Power Standards are *prioritized* standards that are derived from a systematic and balanced approach to distinguishing which standards are absolutely essential for student success from those that are "nice to know." Power Standards are a *subset* of the complete list of standards for each grade and for each subject. They represent the "safety net" of standards each teacher needs to make sure that every student learns prior to leaving the current grade. Students who acquire this "safety net" of knowledge and skills will thus exit one grade better prepared for the next grade.

Once the Power Standards are identified through school and/or district consensus, educators agree to teach these particular standards for depth of student understanding. Curriculum is developed toward that end in each grade level and content area. Meaningful classroom, school, and district assessments are aligned to the Power Standards. These assessments provide the evidence of student attainment of the Power Standards, and students are given multiple opportunities to demonstrate proficiency. The resulting data are systematically collected, examined, reported, and used to improve instruction.

About *Power Standards*

Power Standards presents a proven process for identifying the standards that are most important, a process that can be used successfully with every state's standards in every content area and at every grade level. The book is designed to be a step-by-step, practical manual that educators can use immediately in their own districts to replicate the process that others have successfully followed.

Chapter One presents an in-depth explanation of the rationale for identifying Power Standards. Chapter Two explains the step-by-step process school systems throughout the United States are using to identify their own Power Standards. Because there is a necessity for involving all educators in this important decision-making process, Chapter Three details practical strategies for involving everyone in the identification of Power Standards, whether in an individual school or the entire district.

Chapters Four, Five, and Six provide detailed summaries of the process three different school districts in three different states used to identify their Power Standards, with accompanying commentary by those who directed the work and selected examples of their identified Power Standards. All three districts have generously provided their contact information and website addresses should readers wish to contact them for further information and/or view these districts' Power Standards in their entirety.

The in-depth explanations included in each chapter address the essential questions and issues related to identifying Power Standards. In addition to these explanations, Chapter Seven specifically answers many of the questions most frequently asked when schools and school systems set out to identify their own Power Standards.

Chapter Eight reviews the Power Standards process in a concise, step-by-step checklist format. This checklist can serve as an easy reference for groups of educators as they work through their own identification of Power Standards.

Chapter Nine briefly discusses how Power Standards can be "unwrapped" to determine the concepts and skills students need to know and be able to do in order to better focus instruction and assessment.

In the Appendices section, two informative articles by Dr. Douglas Reeves, "The 'Safety Net' Curriculum," and "Power Standards for the Middle Grades," provide both a summary of the rationale for Power Standards and a succinct illustration of what those Power Standards would look like in the middle grades. These articles can be used as executive summaries when introducing Power Standards to educators.

At the end of selected chapters, a Reader's Assignment is provided to assist readers in immediately applying the information specific to that chapter. Utilizing these Reader's Assignments, educators can successfully identify their own Power Standards by the book's conclusion.

Power Standards will benefit school and district leaders, classroom teachers, curriculum coordinators, and instructional specialists in all content areas. The straightforward and easy-to-read format enables readers to share confidently and apply immediately these proven, practical strategies in their own school and district settings. Educators can thus achieve the goal of significantly improving achievement for *all* students by first identifying the standards that "matter the most"!

CHAPTER ONE

Why Power Standards?

A Formidable Set of Challenges

School systems throughout the nation today face a formidable set of challenges. Three of these challenges in particular relate directly to state standards.

First, many students are not learning at levels high enough to demonstrate proficiency on standards-based state assessments.

Secondly, the standards at each grade level often contain more concepts and skills than students can realistically learn within the course of one school year. Educators who are given no strategies for managing the volume of standards must, on their own, "pick and choose" the ones they believe will most benefit their students. This leads to inconsistencies as to which standards are emphasized and which are not. Such an approach can negatively impact student performance on high stakes assessments if the "wrong" standards are targeted. To safeguard this from happening, educators feel that they must "cover" *all* the standards with less than optimum depth.

Lastly, educators believe their academic freedom to make professional decisions about what their students need to learn is being eclipsed in what they perceive to be a move toward *standardization*, rather than an effective implementation of *standards* to improve both instruction and student achievement.

Power Standards will confront these challenges with common sense solutions that are being implemented successfully by school systems across the country.

Operational Definitions

Let's start with a few key definitions. "***Standards***," as the word is used here, is shorthand for the complete term "academic content standards," the ***general*** *statements* of what students need to know and be able to do. Its companion term, "***indicators***," varies from state to state and has many names—benchmarks, learning outcomes, proficiencies, sub-skills, sub-standards, elements, etc. The definition of the term "*indicators*," however, is consistent from state to state—the ***grade-specific*** learning expectations for students.

"**Power Standards,**" a term coined by Dr. Douglas Reeves of the Center for Performance Assessment, refers to those standards and indicators that are **critical for student success**. By his own definition, Power Standards are "those standards that, once mastered, give a student the ability to use reasoning and thinking skills to learn and understand other curriculum objectives." Dr. Reeves makes an important distinction between the relative importance of standards and indicators by separating all of them into two main categories—in his terms, those that are "essential" and those that are "nice to know."

Power Standards are thus a carefully selected **subset** of the complete list of standards and indicators within each grade level and content area that students need for success.

Respect for State Standards

On July 20, 2001, I was honored to present a keynote address to the U.S. Department of Education's fourth annual *Improving America's Schools Summer Institute* in Washington, D.C. The title of that year's Institute was "Raising Achievement in Low-Performing Schools" and was sponsored by the Department's Turning Around Low-Performing Schools Initiative. Representatives from all 50 states were in attendance.

In my address, entitled, "Powerful Practices to Improve Student Achievement," I discussed Power Standards as one such practice. At its conclusion, a department of education official from one of the states approached the podium to speak with me.

After introducing herself, she said, "I was a little nervous when you began discussing the idea of Power Standards because we believe that students need to learn *all* the standards. But you made a persuasive case for *narrowing* the standards in a balanced and sensible way."

I wish to point out that the ideas presented in this book are not intended in any way to undermine the hard work that has gone into the determination of any state's standards or the published documents that these efforts produced. When state standards committees sat down to identify their academic content and performance standards, the end results represented the collective set of knowledge and skills that its committee members *ideally* would want all of the students in their state to know and be able to do. The issue here is not whether students *should* learn all the concepts and skills embedded in all the state standards, but whether or not this is an achievable goal within the instructional time available in any given school year.

Prioritization, not Elimination

Nor am I advocating the elimination of certain standards and indicators as part of this process. By state law, educators are bound to teach their students all the standards and indicators in their assigned grade level or department. I am instead endeavoring to make the case for *prioritizing* the standards and indicators rather than regarding all of them as being equal in importance.

The other point to make here is that certain states may not need to identify Power *Standards* if they already have a limited number of standards in a particular subject matter area. Indiana, for example, only has seven language arts standards. Ohio, as another example, only has ten. It would be ludicrous to suggest that states such as these narrow still further an already reduced number of standards. A closer look will reveal that the seven Indiana language arts standards and the ten Ohio language arts standards already *are* Power Standards. They represent the critical knowledge and skills students need for success in language arts along the K-12 spectrum of learning. Yet the number of *indicators* listed beneath each standard may be considerable. For these and other states that have organized their standards in a similar way, the term Power *Indicators* may be more appropriate if it is the *indicators* that need prioritization.

So as not to confuse the reader from this point on, I will use the term Power Standards to mean either the prioritized standards *or* the prioritized, grade-specific indicators that any state or district determines to be critical for student success.

The Rationale for Power Standards

There is a convincing rationale for differentiating standards as either "essential" or "nice to know." The consensus among educators nationwide is that in-depth instruction of "essential" concepts and skills is more effective than superficially "covering" every concept in the textbook. Owing to the limitations of time and the wide diversity in learning backgrounds of today's students, teachers are faced with the almost insurmountable task of trying to teach all the standards and indicators for their particular grade and content areas while at the same time meeting the extraordinary range of student learning needs.

When Robert Marzano, noted educational researcher, was asked what conditions were needed to implement standards effectively, he replied, "Cut the number of standards and the content within standards dramatically." He went on to say that in order to teach all the content represented by what he and his associates at the Mid-continent Research for Education and Learning (McREL) Institute in Aurora, Colorado, had calculated as 3,500 benchmarks (indicators) spread across 14 different content areas, "you would have to change schooling from K-12 to K-22. The sheer number of standards is the biggest impediment to implementing standards" (2001).

The "less is more" maxim may point the way to resolving this dilemma. The educational system in the United States has practiced more of an "inch deep and a mile wide" approach to K-12 instruction, which always leads me to ask educators in my workshops, "Wouldn't it better benefit the learning needs of all students if we were to flip that around and adopt an 'inch wide and a mile deep' approach to instruction of the standards identified as 'essential'?"

The usual response I get to this is, "We agree in principle, but that's not what we can do in practice because there are too many standards to cover for the state test."

I counter with, "So you're saying that the state test is now driving instruction?" Heads nod in somber agreement.

A Reality Check

Certainly the rationale that "less is more" makes perfect sense, but the pressure to achieve test scores in today's climate of increased accountability inserts a reality check into such discussions. This dichotomy is represented in the graphic on the next page.

A second-year math educator in an Eastern state confided to me during a workshop based on my co-authored book, *Five Easy Steps To A Balanced Math Program* (2000), that he had just reviewed all the grade-level math standards he was required to teach his students. He was seized by panic to realize that what he had taught to date represented only 60 percent of what his students would need to know for his state's test that was only two months away. I asked him what he was going to do.

He replied, "I've stopped teaching. Now I'm just giving the kids worksheets and practice drills so I can at least cover the rest of the material they will be tested on."

But We Have To Do It *All*!

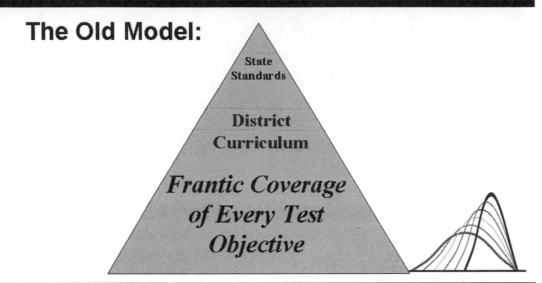

The Old Model:

State Standards

District Curriculum

Frantic Coverage of Every Test Objective

Center for Performance Assessment

When teaching becomes reduced to this kind of high pressure, last-minute test preparation, serious questions arise:

1. What effect does this have on teacher and student motivation?

2. What does this do to the quality of teaching?

3. What impact does this have on student preparation for the next level of learning?

When I ask educators if all of their students came to them prepared to learn their particular grade's standards, the answer is invariably, "No." When I ask them why they think that is the case, they reply with a host of responses that include but are not limited to the following: lack of motivation on the part of the students, high student mobility, second language challenges, complex student learning needs, ineffective instruction in prior grades, etc.

Who Is to Blame Here?

Often to lighten the somber mood these hard questions produce, I will say to the audience, "Aren't high school teachers thinking, 'If only those middle school teachers would do their job, the students would come prepared for high school?'"

Before anyone thinks I'm seriously pointing an accusing finger, I immediately ask, "And what are middle school teachers thinking about all this? That if only those elementary teachers had just done *their* job, right?

"Well, what do you think the upper elementary teachers are saying? You guessed it! If only those primary teachers had prepared the kids for the demands of the upper elementary curriculum!"

"And it doesn't stop there! What do you imagine the primary teachers are saying?"

The audience immediately answers, "It's the parents' fault!"

Amid the ensuing laughter, everyone acknowledges how often, out of frustration, we "blame" the teaching that came before us when, in truth, everyone is doing the very best they can do each year. Certainly there are numerous factors that contribute to the fact that our students are not completely prepared for each new grade. Many of these factors are beyond our individual or collective control. We need to identify probable causes we *can* control and address those in a systematic way.

One Cause We Can Control

If instruction each year is reduced to racing students through an "inch-deep" coverage of standards, surely this must be one of the main reasons why students often do not remember what they learned last year. The resulting lack of readiness for the current year's standards thus necessitates a time-consuming review and re-teaching of concepts and skills that students "should have learned" in prior grades. The cumulative effect of this cycle being repeated over several years begs the question, "Unless we change the way we teach the standards, how can we ever expect to see different results?"

By emphasizing depth over breadth, we can do much to help students retain what they have been taught. With this frame of reference, educators can provide learning experiences around a *prioritized* set of standards and indicators that require students to utilize higher-order thinking skills and integrate present learning with prior knowledge.

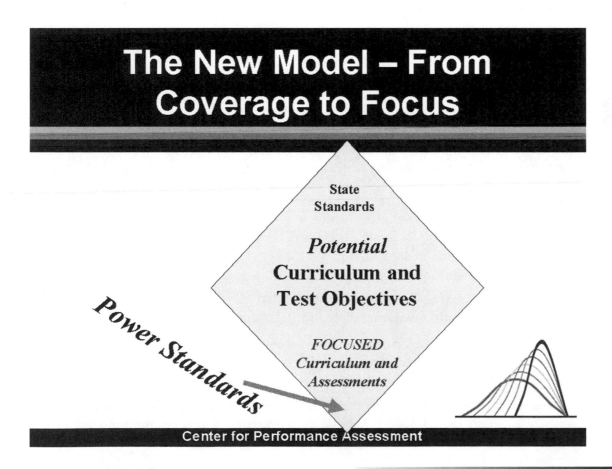

The New Model – From Coverage to Focus

State Standards

Potential Curriculum and Test Objectives

FOCUSED Curriculum and Assessments

Power Standards

Center for Performance Assessment

Rather than perpetuating any longer the old model of "frantic coverage of every standard and every tested objective," what about the preceding model as a better alternative?

"Punt the Rhombus"

Dr. Douglas Reeves gives an illustration which he calls "Punt the Rhombus" to show how a Midwestern state's 87 middle school math standards were reorganized into the following seven Power Standards.

1. *All four number operations (add, subtract, multiply, divide) with and without calculators*

2. *Two-dimensional scale drawings*

3. *Transform a word problem into an accurate picture representation of the problem*

4. *Fraction, decimal, and percentage operations (add, subtract, multiply, divide)*

5. *Measurement in standard and metric units*

6. *Graphs, charts, tables (create them from raw data, and draw inferences from them when presented)*

7. *Properties of rectangles and triangles.*

Certainly this short list represents more than seven standards, but it does broadly define the major concepts and skills that middle school students need to know and be able to do in order to be mathematically literate. All the other standards are not excluded, but there remains a relentless focus on getting every student proficient in these seven standards.

To reorganize the standards as Dr. Reeves did in the above example, consider using these two guiding questions:

1. What essential understandings and skills do our students need?

2. Which standards can be clustered or incorporated into others?

When I share the "Punt the Rhombus" illustration in my Power Standards workshops, I direct everyone's attention to number seven on the list, *Properties of rectangles and triangles.*

I then ask, "If you only had two weeks left in the school year to teach students who had just transferred into your class, which would have more long-term value, leverage, and practicality for those students—knowing how to find the area and perimeter of rectangles and triangles or memorizing the formula for finding the area of a rhombus, parallelogram, or trapezoid?"

It is obvious to most that the former is far more likely to be a necessary life skill and to appear more frequently on state tests than the latter.

"So we 'punt' the rhombus, which means we categorize that standard or indicator as one that is 'nice to know' rather than 'essential'."

It is important to note, however, that students who thoroughly understand the properties of rectangles and triangles ("essentials") and know how to find the area and perimeter of both would also be better able to demonstrate the same knowledge and skills with regard to a rhombus, parallelogram, and trapezoid. The latter geometric shapes can then be taught *in the context* of rectangles and triangles, but the clear distinction is made as to which is more important and which deserves greater instructional emphasis.

All Standards Must Be Taught

Let me reiterate: Identifying Power Standards does *not* relieve teachers of the responsibility for teaching *all* the standards and indicators in the grade level or curricular area they have been assigned to teach. What is necessary is to make the important distinction—*which* standards are critical for student success, and which *other ones* can be given less emphasis, taught and assessed as they relate to the concepts and skills within the identified Power Standards.

While educators embrace the idea of prioritizing the standards, some are still concerned that if certain standards and indicators are singled out as Power Standards, what will happen to the "nice to know" standards and indicators? If these are de-emphasized to the point where educators only focus on the Power Standards, will educators run the risk of eventually neglecting to teach them altogether, thereby creating gaps in student learning needed in later years? And what impact would this have on state test scores?

Two California Solutions

Anticipating this potential problem, administrators in two California school districts that I have worked with came up with a sensible solution.

Jim Fuller, Director of Assessment for the Newark Unified School District in Newark, California, proposed a method of placing a checkmark next to the standards that district educators had determined as "power" or "essential." In this way teachers would be able to see the entire list of California standards for which they were responsible, but know that the ones that were checked needed to be taught for depth of understanding.

Jim told me, "The need to identify 'essential' standards began as we considered the core knowledge and skills our high school students need to pass the California High School Exit Exam. I reorganized the standards by placing each one under broad, overarching statements of what students need to know and be able to do. Then I looked at each of the standards beneath those overarching statements and determined which ones were 'essential' for students to know and be able to do in order to achieve that particular overarching statement. For example, under the broader skill of writing a narrative essay, I listed the specific standards that relate to vocabulary skills, organization skills, spelling skills, etc. I recognized that these overarching skill statements could serve as the focus for the development of performance assessments aligned to the 'essential' standards and could eventually lead to the development of a revised, standards-based report card."

Jim Armstrong, former principal of Righetti High School and current Assistant Superintendent of Curriculum and Instruction in the Santa Maria Joint Union High School District, Santa Maria, California, shared with me Righetti's method of differentiating the most important standards from the "nice to know" standards in consideration of the high-stakes tests required by the state.

Righetti High School published, for use by its own staff, a document with several columns on legal-sized paper turned horizontally. In the first column appears the full-text of the standards for a particular content area. The Power Standards are bolded and the remaining ("nice to know") standards appear in regular print. In the next two columns, Righetti aligned each standard with the number of items on the California High School Exit Exam and the Stanford 9 (standardized test administered in all grades two through eleven). The final column lists the particular curriculum, lessons, and activities that can be used to teach the targeted Power Standards represented on both exams.

When I asked Jim what the response has been to this document, he replied, "Very positive. Righetti teachers really like the format. They can see at a glance the standards that need to be especially emphasized, what percentage of test items each standard will receive, and the suggested lessons and activities to use for instruction. Of course, now that the Stanford Achievement Test 9 is being replaced with the California Achievement Test 6, Righetti staff may want to revisit these documents and realign the Power Standards with the new state test, but the process we first developed can easily be repeated."

Choosing the "Essential"

At a National School Conference Institute (NSCI) general session I attended in February 2000, in Phoenix, Arizona, Heidi Hayes Jacobs, nationally known educator, author, and consultant, had this to say with regard to effectively managing the standards: "Given the limited time you have with your students, curriculum design has become more and more an issue of deciding what you won't teach as well as what you will teach. You cannot do it all. As a designer, you must choose the essential."

What, exactly, is the "essential?" Educators who have attended my workshops throughout the United States clearly agree that not all standards and indicators are equal in importance, so I ask them to consider how they would define "essential" with regard to the selection of standards. I pose the following question to the more experienced teachers in the audience.

"Who among you has *ever* in one year been able to teach and assess all the standards and indicators for which you are responsible?"

No hands go up; uncomfortable laughter rises in the room instead.

I then ask these seasoned educators, "So how do you decide which standards are the most important ones to teach when you realize there is no way to teach all of them effectively in the time you have?"

They answer, "We pick and choose!"

"Based on what?" I ask.

They call out a variety of responses, such as the following:

"What I like to teach."

"What's on the test."

"What students need for next year."

This invariably sparks animated table discussions. I wait a few moments for the talk to subside and then ask a final question to make my point.

"Are all of you using the same selection criteria?"

The response is a mixture of laughter and groans. Everyone knows that the answer to *that* question is "No!"

How Educators Define "Essential"

In the absence of an agreed-upon set of criteria for prioritizing the standards and indicators, educators will, out of necessity, make up their own. Whether those criteria are implicitly understood or explicitly defined, the following question is uppermost in educators' minds as they consider what to teach their students:

*"What knowledge and skills must I impart to my students **this** year so that they will enter **next** year's class with confidence and a readiness for success?"*

This question is what motivates educators to frequently say to their students, "Now *next* year, you are going to need to know and be able to do such and such." This is their way of forecasting for their students the importance of what they are currently learning as a preparation for future grades while at the same time using that same criterion to emphasize certain standards and indicators over others.

Power Standards Identification Criteria

As common as the above practice may be, all too often it is done by individual educators working in isolation from their colleagues. Educators need to be able to collaborate regularly in order to make the aforementioned question a more explicit and commonly used criterion for effective selection of the most important standards and indicators.

Wouldn't educators welcome a distinct, agreed-upon set of criteria for distinguishing the "essential" standards from those that are "nice to know?" Such a two-tiered differentiation would yield a focused set of standards and indicators essential for student success.

What are these distinct criteria? Dr. Douglas Reeves suggests the following three:

1. ***Endurance*** – Will this standard or indicator provide students with knowledge and skills that will be of value beyond a single test date? For example, proficiency in reading will endure throughout a student's academic career and professional life.

2. ***Leverage*** – Will this provide knowledge and skills that will be of value in multiple disciplines? For example, proficiency in creating graphs, tables, and charts and the ability to draw accurate inferences from them will help students in math, science, social studies, and language arts. The ability to write an analytical and persuasive essay will similarly help students in every academic discipline.

3. ***Readiness for the next level of learning*** – Will this provide students with essential knowledge and skills that are necessary for success in the next grade or the next level of instruction? For example, fourth grade teachers are unanimous that reading comprehension and math facts recall are essential for third graders who wish to enter the fourth grade confidently and pursue fourth grade studies successfully. Those same fourth grade teachers are not unanimous that the ability to assemble a leaf collection, identify dinosaurs, or know the state capitals are required knowledge for entry into fourth grade.

"School, Life, and the State Test"

When I work with educators to identify their Power Standards, I ask a guiding question for Power Standards identification that many have said provided them with the "Aha!" for zeroing in on those standards and indicators that are critical for students to learn:

> "What do your students need for success—in school (this year, next year, and so on), in life, and on your state tests?"

These three criteria—**school, life, and the state test**—are an easy set for people to remember when they begin discussions about how to identify their Power Standards. Educators like the positive emphasis on *student success*. I remind them of our earlier discussion about how experienced educators invariably emphasize particular standards over others when they realize that there is never enough time to teach everything with the depth needed for maximum student learning. Rather than continuing to make up their own criteria (what they personally like to teach, what they think kids need, etc.), the three criteria listed above provide a common filter that everyone can use to identify the Power Standards.

Whether you prefer to use Dr. Reeves' three criteria (endurance, leverage, readiness for the next level of learning) or my own three (school, life, and the state test) is a matter of individual or group choice. Use whichever ones work best for the educators involved. Either set of three will prove effective in determining the Power Standards.

Are These Criteria Equal in Importance?

When I discussed the Power Standards identification criteria with one faculty of elementary educators, a fourth grade teacher spoke up and said, "Certainly school and life are important considerations for identifying Power Standards, but the reality we are facing today is our state test. If the state is more likely to emphasize certain standards over others on the test, then that criterion must carry more weight than the other two."

On a large piece of chart paper, I quickly drew a triple Venn diagram, with one of the circles much larger than the other two. I then labeled the larger circle "State Test" and the other two, "School" and "Life."

Then I said, "This may indeed be the emphasis today, but for the overall success of our students, it is still important to keep in mind what they will need for success in subsequent years of schooling and in life itself. Learning that endures should be an essential criterion that we never lose sight of. If we identify and concentrate on those standards and indicators, isn't it likely that we will also be preparing students to do well on state tests since a majority of test items will reflect those same standards even if the tests change from year to year?"

The "Safety Net" Curriculum

Dr. Douglas Reeves authored two informative articles that provide a succinct rationale for identifying Power Standards along with an illustration of Power Standards for middle school. He refers to the Power Standards as the "Safety Net" curriculum and defines it as "a very limited set of learning objectives organized for each grade and for each subject. It is *not* the total curriculum—just the 'safety net' that every teacher should ensure that every student knows."

In my workshops, I encourage participants to share these articles with colleagues as an "executive summary," an effective way to introduce others to the idea of Power Standards and get the conversations rolling about how a school and/or district can apply these powerful ideas to their own existing standards and curriculum. These two articles are included in the Appendices section of this book.

Questions To Be Addressed

So how does a group of educators begin identifying their own Power Standards? What is the role of the school or district leader? Does every school determine its own Power Standards, or does the district decide the Power Standards that all its schools are to follow? These and other related questions pertaining to the *process* of identifying Power Standards are addressed in the remaining.

CHAPTER TWO

How to Identify Power Standards

Theory is always important for establishing a purpose for activity. But after the rationale for developing Power Standards has been presented and the group has had time to discuss the ideas and issues raised, it is time to put theory into practice. In this chapter, I will share the Center for Performance Assessment process that individual schools and entire school systems around the country have effectively followed to develop their agreed-upon collection of Power Standards.

Determine Power Standards Identification Criteria

Let us revisit the two sets of suggested criteria for identifying the Power Standards presented at the end of Chapter One.

1. Endurance

2. Leverage

3. Readiness for next level of learning

The second set is derived from the guiding question: "*What do your students need for success—in school (this year, next year, and so on), in life, and on your state tests?*"

1. School

2. Life

3. State Test

Rather than seeing the two sets as distinctly different from one another, the following sentence shows how they can be combined into a revised guiding question for identifying Power Standards:

> "*What do your students need for success—in school this year, next year, and so on (leverage; readiness for next levels of learning), in life (endurance), and on your state tests?*"

To focus discussions and help participants agree upon the selection of Power Standards, consider using also the other two guiding questions that were presented in the "Punt the Rhombus" illustration in Chapter One:

1. What essential understandings and skills do our students need?

2. Which standards and/or indicators can be clustered or incorporated into others?

Determine which criteria and guiding questions to use as you prepare to begin the Power Standards identification process.

Beginning the Process

Each of the steps detailed below can be initially accomplished in one full-day workshop. For simplicity's sake, I will present the process for identifying Power Standards in *one* content area only. However, they can be identified in several content areas simultaneously by having representative educators from each separate content area seated together and following the process described below.

When working with a K-12 group, I begin by asking participants to **select the content area** in which they would first like to identify their Power Standards. I then ask everyone to **sit in one of four grade-span groups**, usually K-2, 3-5, 6-8, or 9-12. I encourage everyone present—classroom educators, administrators, curriculum specialists, and all others—to select the grade span they know the best in this particular content area.

To keep the task at hand from becoming overwhelming or unwieldy, I ask everyone to **select a particular section of the content area standards** in which to begin the process. For example, the content area of language arts has four domains: reading, writing, listening, and speaking. Rather than try and identify the Power Standards in all four domains simultaneously, I urge them to select one of the four. After successfully identifying the Power Standards for that first selected domain, groups repeat the same process with the remaining three.

The same can be done in mathematics, where there are typically six or seven math strands. Everyone can begin with one particular strand, such as Number Sense, for example, and then repeat the same process later with the other remaining strands.

The next step is for each grade-span group to **select one grade within their grade span** in which to begin. I ask participants to open their chosen subject matter standards, turn to the one grade they have selected, and **find the one particular section** they decided to start with.

I remind participants to **keep in mind whichever agreed-upon identification criteria they selected** as they complete the first activity. I write their selected criteria and guiding questions on the overhead projector, chalkboard, or on a PowerPoint slide so that they are visible to everyone in the room as they work through the process.

Then I direct the groups to *take the next five minutes and on their own quickly mark* each standard and indicator for this section that *they* consider to be **absolutely essential** for student success in the grade selected. I ask them to please wait to talk to colleagues sitting next to them until after they have finished.

"Just check the ones you think students must know and be able to do, the ones that you consider to be non-negotiable. As you find ones that you're not sure about, mark them quickly with a question mark and move on down the list. Ready? Please begin."

The group sets to work, and the room is silent as people engage in the task. When the five minutes have elapsed, I call the group back together and ask them, "Why am I giving you so little time for something so important? Why not give you ten, fifteen, even twenty minutes to do this?"

Invariably, the response is, "We'd end up with everything checked, and we'd be right back where we started, with too much!"

And that's exactly the point. The longer we think about each one, the more standards we mark, since the standards represent a comprehensive list of the knowledge and skills we want all students to learn in a deep and meaningful way. But if we consider again the notion that not all standards and indicators are equal in importance, and the fact that there are simply not enough days in the school year to teach all of them in an "inch wide, mile deep" manner, then it is clear that we need to prioritize the standards according to the criteria decided. This quick marking of the standards will greatly assist educators in the first step of this prioritization process.

Table Talk

"Now I'd like you to *talk to your colleagues* at the table. Share the standards and indicators that you marked with each other, and note where you agree, where you disagree, where you're not sure. What about the ones with a question mark? Did you cluster or incorporate any standards and indicators into others? If you or one of your colleagues does not have a standard or indicator marked that you consider essential, did s/he see that particular one as being part of another standard that you both selected? The goal is to *reach an initial consensus* of what the Power Standards should be for this particular grade in this particular section."

The room now comes alive with animated conversation as participants *compare their choices and note similarities and differences*. While this discussion is taking place, I walk around the room and listen in on the conversations. Often, what I hear is easy agreement. When there is a difference of opinion, it usually has to do with an individual's different interpretation of what the standard means. One educator will say to another, "I didn't pick that particular standard or indicator because I saw it as being incorporated into this other one." In other words, through discussion, what initially appeared as disagreement was, in fact, merely a different interpretation. In general, educators usually agree on what they deem important for students to learn. They are able to justify their choices with logic and from experience.

When the group as a whole has finished this step in the process, I bring them back together to provide directions for the next step.

Consult Testing Information Guides

Most states provide educators with printed information on either their Department of Education website or in booklet form that describes the type and frequency of questions students will encounter on the actual state assessment. For states using a norm-referenced or criterion-referenced test from a commercial publisher, a testing information guide is often included with the purchased testing materials. Examples of this include the *Stanford 9 Compendium of Tested Skills and Objectives* (Harcourt) and the *CTBS Teacher's Guide to TerraNova* (McGraw-Hill). These documents can be an invaluable tool for identifying Power Standards and need to be made available to participants at this stage of the process, if at all possible. (Note: Testing Information Guides may not be available for individual purchase. Educators may wish to inquire as to the availability of these from their district's central office.)

Consult District or State Test Data

If no such information is available or if this information does not provide enough specificity regarding the concepts and skills tested, utilize school or district item analysis reports of the state test data to inform the Power Standards identification process. This data will provide insights into the type and frequency of items tested. Those standards and indicators that reflect these tested items can then be identified so that participants can decide whether or not they need to be included in their Power Standards based on the frequency of their representation on the state test.

At this point I say to the group, "On this first pass that you've just completed, you prioritized the standards and indicators based on your own opinion and experience. Now, let's spend the next 15 to 30 minutes and **refer to your state's Testing Information Guides and/or your available test data** to see which concepts and skills will be emphasized the most in terms of the number of questions asked. See if the standards and indicators you just selected are the same ones that the state or the test publisher emphasizes the most. **Revise your selections** accordingly on your individual team lists."

Chart Selections for Individual Grades

When the groups have finished revising their lists for the particular grades they are working on, I ask them to **record the identifying numbers and letters** of their selected Power Standards and indicators **on pieces of chart-size paper** labeled with specific grades. Rather than copy the full text of each standard and indicator selected, I suggest they write a synopsis or brief phrase after each number and letter that summarizes the content of the ones selected. This will be helpful for later steps in the process.

Discussing Vertical Alignment

"Great! Now, please put your individual grade charts aside for now. Those of you in the classroom, how often are you able to meet and collaborate with colleagues *within* your own grade or department?"

The responses from the group usually indicate once a week or once a month for grade-level or department meetings.

"How often do you meet and collaborate with colleagues in the grades *below and above* your own?"

Wherever I ask this question, the answer is almost always the same: "Never."

"Would it be helpful for you, as you identify your Power Standards, to collaborate in vertical teams in order to identify the ones for the grades immediately before and after your own?"

"Absolutely!"

The Wayne Township "Safety Net"

"Then I'd like to show you what educators in the Metropolitan School District of Wayne Township, a large district in Indianapolis, Indiana, produced by collaborating with teaching colleagues in the grades above and below their own. They identified their K-12 essential knowledge and skills (Power Standards) from their state language arts standards, which they named their 'Safety Net,' and then produced these cards for each grade."

I hold up a colorful set of 8½ X 11 inch laminated cards for everyone to see.

"On the front of this particular card for grade seven are listed the seven language arts *standards* in Indiana. Under each standard is the one *indicator* that their educators determined is critical for seventh grade students to attain. Now look what's on the back!"

I turn the card over to reveal the identified "Safety Nets" for grades 6 and 8. Invariably, there is audible admiration from the audience as people immediately recognize the value of what Wayne Township has created. An example of this two-sided card appears on the next two pages, reprinted with permission.

I continue with my explanation.

"Recognizing the need not only to identify the 'Safety Net' for each grade but to vertically align each grade's selections with the grades above and below, Wayne Township knew it was absolutely necessary to provide time for educators to have cross-grade discussions in order to make those determinations. Once the 'Safety Nets' were vertically aligned *within* each individual grade span, their final step was to vertically align all four grade spans. The result was a K-12 language arts 'Safety Net' that has been produced on these laminated cards and distributed to everyone."

Wayne Township has replicated the same process under the direction of their district curriculum coordinators in mathematics, social studies, science, foreign language, and physical education. All educators in the district receive the "Safety Net" card(s) for the particular content areas they teach.

Wayne Township deliberately identified very few indicators for each content area. Since all K-12 educators have been involved in the process, the expectation is that each educator at every grade level will assume "instructional responsibility" for the particular indicators identified for that grade. In this way, educators can indeed teach their "assigned" indicators for depth of student understanding and continue to build on those indicators introduced in prior grades. This will minimize the necessity to re-teach in subsequent years those indicators that students were expected to learn in earlier years.

Chapter Four describes in full the process Wayne Township followed to identify their Power Standards in each of the content areas listed above. Each of their curriculum coordinators has contributed individual commentaries for this book describing how they received input from all educators in the district as part of their process. Copies of the Wayne Township "Safety Nets" are continually requested by school systems across the nation as a model to guide their own Power Standards identification. Wayne Township administrators have generously allowed me to share their website address in Chapter Four for the benefit of readers who wish to review and download their "Safety Nets" as illustrations of their process.

Grade Below and Grade Above

With the stage set for determining vertical alignment, I lead the group through the next step in the process.

"Let's look again at your just-selected Power Standards for the grade you started with. Now you need to **repeat the same process for both the grade below and the grade above**. On your own, spend a few minutes marking the standards and indicators you think are Power Standards for the grade below the one you just completed. Then compare and contrast your list with your colleagues and revise the list based on

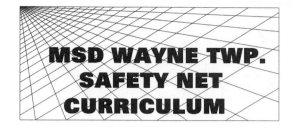

Standard 1 – Word Recognition, Fluency, and Vocabulary Development

7.1.3 – Clarify word meanings through the use of definition, example, restatement, or through the use of contrast stated in the text.

Standard 2 – Reading Comprehension

7.2.3 – Analyze text that uses the cause-and-effect organizational pattern.

Standard 3 – Literary Response and Analysis

7.3.2 – Identify events that advance the plot and determine how each event explains past or present action or foreshadows (provides clues to) future action.

Standard 4 – Writing Process

7.4.2 – Create an organizational structure that balances all aspects of the composition and uses effective transitions between sentences to unify important ideas.

Standard 5 – Writing Applications (Different Types of Writing and Their Characteristics)

7.5.7 – Write for different purposes and to a specific audience or person, adjusting style and tone as necessary.

Standard 6 – Written English Language Conventions

7.6.8 – Use correct capitalization.

Standard 7 – Listening and Speaking

7.7.4 – Arrange supporting details, reasons, descriptions, and examples effectively.

MSD WAYNE TWP.
SAFETY NET CURRICULUM

Standard 1 – Word Recognition, Fluency, and Vocabulary Development

8.1.1 – Analyze idioms and comparisons, such as analogies, metaphors, and similes, to infer the literal and figurative meanings of phrases.

Standard 2 – Reading Comprehension

8.2.4 – Compare the original text to a summary to determine whether the summary accurately describes the main ideas, includes important details, and conveys the underlying meaning.

Standard 3 – Literary Response and Analysis

8.3.6 – Identify significant literary devices, such as metaphor, symbolism, dialect, and irony, which define a writer's style and use those elements to interpret the work.

Standard 4 – Writing Process

8.4.2 – Create compositions that have a clear message, a coherent thesis (a statement of position on the topic), and end with a clear and well-supported conclusion.

Standard 5 – Writing Applications

8.5.1 – Write biographies, autobiographies, and short stories that:
- tell about an incident, event, or situation using well-chosen details.
- reveal the significance of, or the writer's attitude about, the subject.
- use narrative and descriptive strategies, including relevant dialogue, specific action, physical description, background description, and comparison or contrast of characters.

Standard 6 – Written English Language Conventions

8.6.1 – Use correct and varied sentence types (simple, compound, complex, and compound-complex) and sentence openings to present a lively and effective personal style.

Standard 7 – Listening and Speaking

8.7.12 – Deliver research presentations that:
- define a thesis (a position on the topic).
- research important ideas, concepts, and direct quotations from significant information sources and paraphrase and summarize important perspectives on the topic.
- use a variety of research sources and distinguish the nature and value of each.
- present information on charts, maps, and graphs.

MSD WAYNE TWP.
SAFETY NET CURRICULUM

Standard 1 – Word Recognition, Fluency, and Vocabulary Development

6.1.2 – Identify and interpret figurative language (including similes, comparisons that use like or as, and metaphors, implied comparisons) and words with multiple meanings.

Standard 2 – Reading Comprehension

6.2.4 – Clarify an understanding of texts by creating outlines, notes, diagrams, summaries, or reports.

Standard 3 – Literary Response and Analysis

6.3.6 – Identify and analyze features of themes conveyed through characters, actions, and images.

Standard 4 – Writing Process

6.4.3 – Write informational pieces of several paragraphs that:
- engage the interest of the reader.
- state a clear purpose.
- develop a topic with supporting details and precise language.
- conclude with a detailed summary linked to the purpose of the composition.

Standard 5 – Writing Applications

6.5.2 – Write descriptions, explanations, comparison and contrast papers, and problem and solution essays that: state the thesis (purpose on the topic) or purpose; explain the situation; organize the composition clearly; offer evidence to support arguments and conclusions.

Standard 6 – Written English Language Conventions

6.6.1 – Use simple sentences, compound sentences, and complex sentences; use effective coordination and subordination of ideas, including both main ideas and supporting ideas in single sentences, to express complete thoughts.

Standard 7 – Listening and Speaking

6.7.3 – Restate and carry out multiple-step oral instructions and directions.

the Test Information Guide and/or your test data. Reach initial consensus and record your selections on another sheet of chart-size paper. Then repeat the process one more time with the grade above the one you started with. When this is accomplished, we will be ready to discuss vertical alignment."

The groups start buzzing with activity and before long the grade-span charts are completed.

Looking for the Vertical "Flow"

"Next we'll look for the vertical alignment between the grades within your own grade span. If you will please *post your three grade-level charts on the wall in order*, beginning with K-2 on the far left, followed by 3-5, and so on, we can *look for the vertical flow within and between the grade spans*."

The 13 individual grade-level charts go up, and I inform the participants that in a few minutes, I'll ask one or more members from each grade span group to stand next to the charts and provide for the entire K-12 group a brief narrative about their identified Power Standards and what they discovered while working through the selection process. But first I want to provide them all with a focus for listening to each group's sharing, as described in the next section.

Gaps, Overlaps, and Omissions

In assisting school systems in the development of curriculum maps, Heidi Hayes Jacobs, president of Curriculum Designers, Inc., uses a series of terms, "gaps, overlaps, and omissions" to ensure that curriculum is not heavily repeated or inadvertently omitted from one grade to another (1997).

In the identification of Power Standards, it is also particularly important at this step to *look for and identify any gaps, overlaps, and omissions*. Is there a particular standard or indicator needing to be taught to students in more than one grade that is missing from a particular grade's list (a gap)? Is there a certain standard or indicator that is being redundantly taught in two or three grades that could be thoroughly taught in only one grade (an overlap)? Is there a particular standard or indicator likely to be state-tested that is completely missing from one or more grades (an omission)?

I advise the entire group to be on the alert for these as they listen to each grade-span group's narrative. To illustrate the importance of doing so, I share a story about an elementary school faculty I worked with that had decided to first identify Power Standards in mathematics.

One Faculty's Discovery of a Major Omission

Under the direction of their principal, each grade had met together and followed the Power Standards identification process described above. But they had not yet had the vertical discussions with the grade levels above and below their own. When I returned for my second visit with the faculty at an after-school staff meeting, I asked them to select one particular strand of mathematics that each of their grades could use as a model for building vertical alignment in the other math strands. They decided upon geometry.

I said, "Please list the Power Standards you have selected for geometry at your grade level on a piece of large chart paper. As soon as you are finished, each grade level will post their list in order from kindergarten to grade five and share their process with the rest of us. We will listen and look for any gaps, overlaps, or omissions as the charts go up."

The groups got busy and in a few minutes, I asked the kindergarten teachers to share with the faculty which geometry indicators they had selected and why. They posted their chart on the wall, named the two or three indicators they had selected, and then sat down. The first grade teachers then shared their list of geometry indicators, also short. Things were moving along beautifully!

Now the second grade teachers got up, taped their *blank* chart to the wall, and announced, "We have so many other math indicators in the other math strands that we think are more important than geometry. So we really don't teach geometry that much."

I didn't say anything, nor did the rest of the faculty, and the second grade team sat down. The third grade stood up, echoed the same rationale that the second grade team had offered, and posted their chart. It too was blank.

The fourth grade team could barely contain themselves. They immediately jumped up and posted their chart for all to see. On it were listed several geometry indicators.

They announced, "Do you know how many geometry problems there are on the fourth grade state test? We looked at the released tests from the last two years along with the Testing Information Guide to help us identify which indicators in the geometry strand are most likely to be on the next state test. These are critical for our students to learn if they are going to succeed."

In many states, annual testing is conducted only in certain benchmark years, not in every single grade. In this particular state, the first high stakes test is administered in grade four.

Seeking to ease the tensions in the room, I interjected a question for the entire staff.

"Is the fourth grade test only a fourth grade test, or is it a K-4 test?"

As everyone acknowledged that it was the latter, the fourth grade team said to their colleagues, "There is no way we can teach all the tested geometry concepts and skills in our grade alone. We need all of you in K-3 to introduce and develop essential geometric concepts that we can build upon and extend prior to their taking the state test in fourth grade."

The second and third grade teams immediately realized that if they did not do their part to help their students develop an understanding of geometry concepts listed in the second and third grade indicators, the children would not be ready for fourth grade geometry—and the test scores would reflect that.

Immediately, both of those grade-level groups took down their charts from the wall and opened their math standards to the geometry strand in order to revise their list of Power Standards. The principal beamed, and the rest of the staff applauded. In a few minutes, the revised charts from grades two and three were back up on the wall, and we continued the discussion about vertical alignment.

Grade-span Share Out

The above story's message provides the necessary lens through which to examine the grade-span charts that are now posted on the wall. As each grade-span group takes its turn sharing their lists, the large group focuses on whether the identified standards and indicators build vertically. They are on the lookout for any gaps, overlaps, or omissions.

This is where it is helpful to have the eyes of the entire K-12 group scrutinizing the lists. Sometimes educators in other grade-span teams can be more objective in spotting a need for revision that might otherwise go unnoticed by those who work with those standards each and every day. If any gaps, overlaps, or omissions are noticed by anyone, the team makes note of this for later correction.

When all the grade-span groups finish sharing their lists of proposed Power Standards and have noted any changes they wish to make to close the gaps, remove the overlaps, and eliminate the omissions, I provide the group with the time needed to go back to their tables and **revise both their charts and individual team copies**. They will then have the first draft of their Power Standards for this particular content area section!

But Is This Power Standard Appropriate for My Grade?

Recently an educator voiced concern that although a particular Power Standard was identified in her individual grade level, she did not think it was developmentally appropriate for *all* of her students.

She said to me, "I feel I *have* to teach it, even to those few students who are academically struggling, because this particular standard is not listed in the grade above mine, and I know that it will be important for them to know 'down the road'. It's just beyond what they can *presently* do."

I suggested that she speak with the grade level teachers above her to ask them for help with this situation, saying, "Maybe they would be willing to make sure that it is taught to those individual students when they are more able to grasp it conceptually and demonstrate it skillfully."

These types of discussions may need to take place between educators as part of the Power Standards articulation process so that the standards are not changed, but perhaps the *time* when they are taught for depth of understanding is.

Sequencing the Power Standards

After the grade-span groups make any needed revisions, I call the entire group back together once again.

"There is one additional step you may wish to consider doing at some point before the process is completed. This has to do with scheduling or sequencing the identified Power Standards for instruction and assessment."

I ask the grade-span groups to think about their reporting periods. Whether they follow a quarterly or trimester schedule, **decide which standards should be taught in which individual reporting periods** so that there is a logical progression of when to teach which standards. Math, especially, is hierarchical. Certain concepts and skills must be taught before others if students are to truly understand them. In the same way that school systems develop a scope and sequence for the curricula, a scope and sequence can be determined for the identified Power Standards.

At this point, groups often choose to do a preliminary sequencing of their lists by quarter or trimester. They simply look again at their identified Power Standards and *number them according to which ones need to be taught first, second, and so on*, to promote logical progression of student understanding.

Another Point of View Regarding Sequencing

A middle school science educator in the Midwest recently brought up an excellent point with regard to scheduling the Power Standards by quarter or trimester.

"In science, I continually weave concepts and skills that I taught in an earlier unit into other units. I think it is important for students to see the connections between units of study. To slot certain standards into certain quarters defeats the idea of depth versus breadth and limits me as a science teacher as to when I can teach particular topics. The other problem is that we build our units around our field trips and must schedule our sharing of instructional materials. We need to have the flexibility to teach our units in consideration of all these other factors."

Flexibility, not Restriction

Whether a school or district chooses to sequence the Power Standards by reporting period or not is a matter of local choice and consensus. The essential reason for prioritizing the standards and indicators is to be sure that the most important ones are identified and taught for depth of student understanding. With this shift in emphasis from "coverage to focus," educators find more opportunities to revisit and reemphasize those prioritized standards throughout the year and to help students make standards connections within and between content areas. The broader timeframe of an entire academic school year may better afford educators the flexibility needed to accomplish this.

Power Standards Report Cards

The decision to sequence the Power Standards by quarter or trimester often leads to the revision of district report cards to specify which standards and indicators have been targeted as "essential" and when they will be taught and assessed. Assessments can then be designed for grade levels and content areas that evaluate student understanding of the concepts and skills contained in the Power Standards. These assessments with accompanying scoring guides or rubrics provide the evidence as to what degree of proficiency students have attained relative to the Power Standards and indicators taught in a particular reporting period.

Develop an Action Plan

Whether the same large group needs to meet again to continue the Power Standards identification process for the remaining standards in the same content area or to begin the process in other ones, discussion inevitably turns to the matter of developing an action plan for presenting the information about Power Standards to all educators in the school district. This discussion will also include the need for involving all educators in the selection process.

If the group will not be meeting together again, I encourage participants to brainstorm what their next steps should be in introducing this information to their own schools, departments, or districts. The workshop activities of the day have familiarized participants with the *process*, but now they need to think about how to share that process with their colleagues at their own sites.

The next chapter offers effective methods for implementing this process smoothly in either of the above circumstances. It also discusses the differing roles of the principal, department chair, curriculum coordinator, and central office in developing Power Standards.

Reader's Assignment

Using the process outlined above, develop your own first draft of Power Standards in the content area of your choice. Refer again to the bolded, italicized phrases in this chapter to refresh your memory of the steps in the process. You may also wish to refer to Chapter Eight for a more concise, step-by-step checklist to reference as you work through the entire process.

CHAPTER THREE

Involving Everyone in the Process

Whether those present at the Power Standards workshop are principals, assistant principals, department chairs, classroom teachers, instructional specialists, curriculum coordinators, or central office administrators, everyone agrees that for this process to work most effectively, *all the other educators* within a particular school or district need to be involved. In this chapter, I will share effective ways in which educators can best introduce both the rationale and process for identifying the Power Standards to those who were *not* present.

Getting Buy-In

As participants prepare to work on their action plans for introducing these ideas to colleagues, I ask them, "What would happen if you took back the work you have done today, gave a brief explanation to educators in your building or district, and just handed them these drafts? Would they be thrilled and immediately start planning instruction and assessment around these Power Standards?"

The answer I receive is, "A few would, but what would more likely happen is they would be put on the shelf."

"And why is that?"

"Because if people don't have ownership in the task, the outcome or product doesn't have much meaning."

Carefully planning for the involvement of all stakeholders will distinguish a well-implemented idea from a poorly implemented one. Maybe it will not be your responsibility to lead the charge in developing Power Standards for your school or district. But the following information should assist those administrators and educators who *are* assigned that role.

Starting with the School Administrator(s) or Department Chair(s)

Many times this process begins randomly in a particular grade level or within an individual department of a school. Individuals return from the Power Standards workshop and want to immediately identify the Power Standards for the subjects they themselves teach. As more and more faculty members learn about the process, different grades or departments begin working together to determine Power Standards for their particular content areas. Rather than wait for this "grass roots" approach to eventually take hold in all grades and/or departments, here are ways school administrator(s) and department chairs(s) can share the Power Standards information with everyone at the same time.

In an *elementary* building, the principal presents the information at a staff meeting, asks the faculty which content area they would like to start with, organizes them by grade level, and takes them through the complete process described in Chapter Two. S/he then develops with the entire faculty or grade-level representatives a timeline for completion and provides the needed support so that each grade level can meet at specific times to complete the task. When finished, the principal and faculty can repeat the entire process in the next curricular area of choice. The selection of Power Standards for the second curricular area will take less time than the first since everyone is now familiar with the process.

In a *secondary* building, either the principal or assistant principal presents the information to the entire faculty or the department chairs share the information with their colleagues at department meetings. The individual departments then decide where and when to meet as a group to determine their own content area Power Standards.

If the departments are large, sub-groups can be formed according to courses and grades within that discipline. For example, the history department can organize itself according to government, economics, world or U.S. history, etc., and the department members who teach those particular courses can work together to identify the Power Standards for those same courses. In this way, all the Power Standards can be simultaneously identified in a relatively short amount of time and then compiled in a master document for reference by the entire department.

If the departments are small, all the educators in that department can work together to decide which course or grade to begin with, determine the Power Standards for that course or grade, and then simply repeat the process for the remaining courses and grades. In the science department, for example, the Power Standards could first be decided for life science, next for earth science, then for physical science, etc. until all of the science standards for all courses and grades are determined. It may take longer this way since the same group of educators must do all the work, but everyone involved will have the "big picture" of which standards the group thinks are most important and how each course's Power Standards connect to the other ones.

However educators organize themselves to work through this process, the value of the ensuing discussions cannot be underestimated. Not only will everyone be analyzing the standards and indicators "in depth," related conversations about ways to teach and assess the standards more effectively cannot help but take place. Long after these initial discussions conclude, the resulting improvements in instruction and student learning will continue.

Starting with the Curriculum Coordinators

One or more curriculum coordinators from a particular school district often attend the Power Standards workshop together. As they work through the activities, they discuss with each other how to identify Power Standards in their respective subject matter areas simultaneously so as to expedite the process district-wide.

The curriculum coordinators usually start by brainstorming a list of names of educators from different buildings who are experienced and highly competent in their particular content areas. They discuss inviting these individuals to a district meeting in order to tap their expertise and assistance in the identification of Power Standards. They decide when to schedule meetings with those individuals and plan timelines for completion of the work.

There are several benefits to beginning the Power Standards process with the district curriculum coordinators:

1. These leaders can invite a broad spectrum of content area experts in several disciplines to become part of the process, thus recognizing the experience and expertise of those individual educators.

2. The curriculum coordinators can share the initial information with all of these experts in the same place at the same time, ensuring that everyone hears a consistent message.

3. They can receive the valuable input from these curricular experts as they work through the Power Standards selection process together, rather than relying solely on their own judgment.

4. They can then immediately schedule separate follow-up meetings for each curricular group to complete the process, if needed.

5. First drafts of the Power Standards can thus be completed in several disciplines in a fraction of the time it would take to finish the work in one content area before beginning it in another.

Starting with the Central Office Administrators

It takes time for a new practice or methodology, however effective it may be, to make its way through an entire school district. When central office administrators attend the Power Standards workshop, they are thinking of the most strategic ways to implement these ideas across the district. Whether that work is begun at individual schools that will be most receptive to the practice or at district meetings attended by representatives from different buildings, central office administrators know that eventually three challenges must be addressed: 1) how to identify Power Standards in *every* targeted content area; 2) how to implement the identified Power Standards in *every* building in the district; and 3) how to involve *all* educators in the process for maximum effectiveness.

Regardless of how, where, and to what degree the process begins within a district, the next critical steps are to share the information with everyone, create first drafts of Power Standards in selected content areas, receive feedback from all district educators about those drafts, and then revise those drafts to reflect that feedback.

Central Office administrators can accomplish this by enlisting the help of their curriculum coordinators to schedule one or more district meetings—however many are needed to complete the tasks outlined below—and then invite representatives from each of the buildings to be a part of the process. If any buildings have already drafted their own set of Power Standards in one or more content areas and/or grade levels, the curriculum coordinators ask those representatives to bring their drafts to the meeting.

11-Step Agenda for District Meeting(s)

The agenda for the district meeting(s) can be set as follows:

1. Establish purpose of the meeting—identification of a common set of Power Standards for one or more subject matter areas reflective of the combined input from educators across the district.

2. Briefly explain the rationale for identifying Power Standards.

3. Divide attendees into grade-span configurations.

4. Review any drafts of identified Power Standards submitted from participating buildings. If none are submitted, grade-span colleagues create a first draft for the content area(s) of choice.

5. For those groups with first drafts from different buildings, create a *second* draft of Power Standards that reflects the combined input from those sites.

6. Check the first (and second) drafts for vertical alignment within the grade span, and reference the state's Testing Information Guide and/or district item analysis reports of test data. Make any further revisions necessary.

7. Publish drafts for review by educators in all buildings.

8. Individual faculties review the new district drafts of Power Standards, provide feedback, and offer any further suggestions for revision.

9. Building representatives return to the next district Power Standards meeting with their site feedback and any proposed revisions.

10. They review commentary from sites and make final revisions that reflect the latest feedback. (Districts may choose to ask sites to critique these final revisions one last time before publication).

11. Final drafts of the Power Standards are published and distributed to all sites.

The Accordion Model

Dr. Douglas Reeves named this series of steps to include all educators in the district, "The Accordion Model," using the metaphor of an accordion's outward and inward movement of its bellows to illustrate involving all educators in the identification of the Power Standards.

First, representatives from the individual buildings take drafts of their own Power Standards to the initial district meeting (accordion in). The participants incorporate the collective input received from the sites into new drafts and then send them back to the buildings for review (accordion out). The sites provide feedback, offer any remaining suggestions for revision, and return the drafts once again to the district (accordion in). Revisions and suggestions are incorporated into final drafts that are then published and distributed to all sites.

There is a persuasive rationale for having such an organizational plan ready to implement. As individual schools hear about Power Standards and begin identifying their own, sooner or later someone will ask the logical questions, "Why are we identifying our own Power Standards when they may be different from those determined by other schools in our district? Won't this create inconsistencies rather than minimize them?"

The Accordion Model, or any other effective plan, resolves those differences, honors the input and feedback of all educators, and thus promotes a much broader acceptance of the final product(s).

A related question often raised is, "Why should individual schools do the work of identifying their own Power Standards if the goal is to eventually determine *district* Power Standards? Why not just begin the whole process at the district level?"

This can be accomplished by "playing" the Accordion Model in reverse order. Curriculum coordinators working with building representatives at a district meeting create and send first drafts to the sites (accordion out). The sites review the first drafts, provide feedback, offer suggestions for revision, and send the drafts back to the district (accordion in). Second drafts reflecting the feedback received are distributed again to the sites for further suggestions and/or approval (accordion out). Once that feedback is returned and reviewed (accordion in), final drafts incorporating any suggested revisions are then published and distributed to all sites. Often this latter method is exactly how the process begins, especially if the Power Standards information has first been heard by a central office administrator or by curriculum coordinators who are considering the entire district in all their decisions.

Reasons for Beginning Process at School Sites

If a district is large and not yet ready to begin this work on such a grand scale, individual schools eager to identify their Power Standards may not want to wait for the process to be initiated at the district level. Many times I have heard building level administrators express their hope that the district will eventually embrace this practice, but they decide that it needs to take place right away at their own sites. They see the identification of Power Standards as a powerful strategy for effectively prioritizing the standards, getting all staff "on the same page" as to what is truly important for students to know and be able to do, and immediately targeting those standards most heavily emphasized on the state test.

A Preview: Three Districts from Three States

To illustrate how the ideas described thus far have been successfully applied in school systems across the country, the next three chapters provide detailed summaries of the process three different school districts in three different states used to identify their Power Standards, with accompanying commentary by those who directed the work and selected examples of their identified Power Standards. All three districts have kindly provided their contact information and website addresses should readers wish to contact them for further information and/or view these districts' Power Standards in their entirety.

Remaining Questions

There are certain to be additional questions that arise as readers consider this information and its implementation within their own particular school systems. The narration given in the three district chapters that follow will hopefully answer many of the remaining questions readers may have about how to implement these ideas. To further assist readers, please refer to Chapter Seven, in which Dr. Douglas Reeves and I present a list of the questions most frequently asked regarding Power Standards and our responses to those queries.

Reader's Assignment

How can you introduce the Power Standards process to your school, department, curriculum committee, or district? Develop an action plan using the following questions as guidelines to get you thinking about the most effective way to both share this information and to involve all educators in the process. You may wish to refer again to the proposed agenda provided earlier in this chapter for district meeting(s) to determine Power Standards as well as the step-by-step checklist for identifying Power Standards in Chapter Eight.

1. Who needs to hear this information first?

2. When will it be shared?

3. Which content area(s) should we begin with?

4. What should be our timeframe for completion?

5. Which version of the Accordion Model would work best in our district? Start with schools first, then take them to the district, then back to schools OR start with the district, send drafts to schools for feedback, and return them to the district for revision and publication?

CHAPTER FOUR

Wayne Township, Indianapolis, Indiana

The Metropolitan School District of Wayne Township, a large district in the West Central portion of Marion County, adjacent to the Indianapolis International Airport, Indianapolis, Indiana, created their first collection of Power Standards in language arts during the 2000-01 school year. The process and end results were so well-received by district administrators, building leaders, and classroom educators that plans were soon made to identify Power Standards in other content areas. To date, MSD Wayne Township has identified Power Standards in language arts, mathematics, science, social studies, physical education, and foreign language.

The district's leadership team under the visionary direction of Dr. Terry Thompson, superintendent, and Dr. Karen Gould, assistant superintendent, first learned the rationale for Power Standards from Dr. Douglas Reeves, founder of the Center for Performance Assessment. Dr. Reeves referred to Power Standards as the "Safety Net," a very limited set of learning objectives organized for each grade and for each subject that every teacher should ensure every student knows.

Dr. Karen Gould provided the following statement attesting to the value of Power Standards:

> "Our efforts to focus our teachers on using the standards to drive instruction and assessment would not have gone as smoothly as it has if it were not for our establishment of the Power Standards for every core discipline. The process of developing the Power Standards was an important first step in helping our teachers embrace standards as *the* focus of their teaching. When you have over 900 teachers, as Wayne Township does, that can seem like a daunting task, but we created a system that directly involved each teacher in the process of determining the Power Standards. Now, teachers have their 'Safety Nets' close by when developing their teaching plans and their assessments. Students and parents know what our Power Standards are and see them represented in our newly revised, standards-based reporting system."

K-12 Language Arts "Safety Net"

Language Arts was the first content area to identify Power Standards. The process began under the direction of Carole Erlandson, Language Arts Coordinator, K-12. In late summer of 2000, Carole communicated with me by phone and e-mail to plan out the process she was about to use with her language arts grade-level representatives. In the following pages, Carole summarizes the process she followed:

"The district holds a K-12 district articulation day twice each school year. All certified teachers from all 15 schools meet together for professional development during the afternoon of an early release day. In the elementary schools, each grade level teacher represents one of the main core subject areas. For example, if there are four grade two teachers, one teacher represents language arts, one represents mathematics, one represents science, and one represents social studies. If there is a fifth teacher, s/he joins the language arts area. At the junior high and high school levels, all the teachers in each department join the elementary representatives for cross-grade sharing and collaboration in curriculum planning.

"On the first articulation day during the fall of 2000, I chaired a meeting that was attended by a grade-level language arts representative from each of our ten elementary schools and all the junior and senior high school English and language arts teachers. We discussed the fact that each of Indiana's seven language arts standards represented broad knowledge and skills necessary for our students to learn. Then we explained the reasons why we needed to devise a way to narrow our grade-specific indicators since there were simply too many to teach and assess adequately each year. To identify our language arts 'Safety Net,' we presented the idea of using three selection criteria—what our students needed to succeed in school, in life, and on the Indiana Statewide Testing for Educational Progress Plus (ISTEP+)."

Grade-Span Groups

Carole continues, "The next step was to group the K-12 representatives into grade-span groups. Since our elementary schools include grades K-6, our junior high schools include grades 7-9, and our high school includes grades 10-12, we organized everyone according to K-3, 4-6, 7-9, and 10-12. These groups were made up of about eight to ten teachers each. Because of the large number of teachers present, there were multiple groups for each grade span. The focus for discussion was on selecting the most important indicators under each of the seven standards in language arts, using the 'school, life, and the test' selection criteria, and vertically aligning those indicators across grade levels. The selection of the 'Safety Net' indicators was based on what the teachers decided would provide the best instructional focus needed to meet our state's testing program in grades three, six, eight, and ten.

"When all the grade span groups finished their initial selections, the entire K-12 group met again to share each grade span's proposed 'Safety Net' indicators with everyone else. The process worked!

"Even though this was a new and uncertain experience for our language arts representatives, there was a wonderful spirit of collaboration evident throughout the entire process.

Involving **Every** *Teacher in the Process*

"Grace Meyer, my secretary, compiled and sent out to all school sites each grade-span's 'Safety Net' recommendations along with the entire list of language arts indicators.

"It was important that all teachers throughout the district understood the purpose of the 'Safety Net,' the need for articulation between each grade span, and the progression of learning represented by the selected 'Safety Net' indicators. Each of the grade level language arts representatives was responsible for sharing with all other teachers at their grade level the information about the 'Safety Net' and how the sample selection process had taken place.

"*Every* teacher in Wayne Township was then asked to review the provided list of language arts indicators for his or her particular grade level and select his or her first, second, and third choice for the *one* 'Safety Net' indicator s/he thought to be absolutely essential for student understanding. The schools were asked to collect and send this information back to my office. This was a *major* effort, and we diligently sought this feedback from any school or teacher whose response we had not received. We felt it was absolutely necessary to get the 'Safety Net' priority indicators from *all* certified staff."

Organizing Teacher Choices, Reaching Consensus, Publishing Results

Carole continues, "We then placed this collected information on a spreadsheet. The three different choices for each grade level from each school were plotted to clearly show which indicators had been ranked first, second and third by all certified staff. The results of this input led to the final decision of the 'Safety Net' indicators for all seven state standards in language arts. Our 'Safety Net' for language arts truly represents a consensus of *all* Wayne Township teachers.

"The 'Safety Net' indicators were printed in a color-coded, user-friendly format and laminated on 8 ½ x 11 inch cardstock so that teachers could easily reference them for lesson planning."

(Author's Note: Carole and her committee had the great idea to make the laminated cards two-sided, as mentioned and illustrated in Chapter Two. Listed on the front of the card are the 'Safety Net' indicators for a particular grade. Listed on the back of the card are the 'Safety Net' indicators for both the grade *below* and the grade *above*. In this way, teachers can see which indicators preceded and succeeded the ones they are assigned to teach at their particular grade levels).

Assessment, Alignment, Parents, and Report Cards

"This process worked, and *most* teachers are in agreement with the results. Our language arts representatives wanted to keep working with the 'Safety Net' and adjusting the indicators, but we moved on to conversations regarding assessment and how teachers can work with the 'Safety Net' to assure that teaching and testing match and are in alignment with the prioritized indicators. Because our language arts representatives are available throughout the year at their schools, they can assist other teachers in clarifying how to use the 'Safety Net' indicators to meet the standards.

"Parents have been informed that the 'Safety Net' represents the top priorities in their students' learning. The district now has a report card for parents using the 'Safety Net' indicators to assess the progress of all students at the elementary grades. We are still in the process of making our formative and summative assessments the best they can be."

Numerous Benefits

Carole continues, "The great benefit to working through this process was the way it got teachers *into* the standards, how it raised their awareness level about the standards. The cross-grade discussions were the best by-product. The *process* of selecting the 'Safety Net' indicators was so valuable, maybe even more so than the final product itself.

"District test scores on our state ISTEP+ assessments and our off-year *TerraNova* assessments have been proof of the benefits of focusing and prioritizing our many state standard indicators into the 'Safety Net.' Our teachers study the test score data and adjust instruction to meet the needs of our students.

"There have been other benefits in student learning, too. The students are now aware of the focus on certain indicators, and teachers are posting them in their classrooms. The same language and vocabulary is now being used across grade levels, and students are making connections from one grade to the next.

Updating the "Safety Net"

Carole concludes, "This fall (2002), our state test (ISTEP+) will be changing the items on the test to reflect the state standards. We plan to revisit our Power Standards identification process and revise the 'Safety Net' after we receive the results of our student performance on ISTEP+ later this fall. We consider the 'Safety Net' a work in progress and hope that teachers will continue to make suggestions to improve our process, but everyone agrees that remaining consistent and focused on the identified indicators is our top priority."

Included below are selected examples from the Wayne Township K-12 language arts "Safety Net," reprinted with permission.

Safety Net Skills for
Language Arts Standards

GRADE 3

Standard 1 – Word Recognition, Fluency, and Vocabulary Development

3.1.6 Use sentence and word context to find the meaning of unknown words.

Standard 2 – Reading Comprehension

3.2.4 Recall major points in the text and make and revise predictions about what is read.

Standard 3 – Literary Response and Analysis

3.3.4 Determine the theme or author's message in fiction and non-fiction text.

Standard 4 – Writing Process

3.4.3 Create single paragraphs with topic sentences and simple supporting facts and details.

Standard 5 – Writing Applications

(Different Types of Writing and Their Characteristics)

3.5.2 Write descriptive pieces about people, places, things, or experiences that: develop a unified main idea; use details to support the main idea.

Standard 6 – Written English Language Conventions

3.6.2 Write correctly complete sentences of statement, command, question, or exclamation, with final punctuation. Declarative, imperative, interrogative, and exclamatory.

Standard 7 – Listening and Speaking

3.7.3 Answer questions completely and appropriately.

MSD Wayne Township, Indianapolis, IN
Safety Net Skills for
Language Arts Standards

GRADE 4

Standard 1 – Word Recognition, Fluency, and Vocabulary Development

4.1.2 Apply knowledge of synonyms (words with the same meaning), antonyms (words with opposite meaning), homographs (words that are spelled the same but have different meanings), and idioms (expressions that cannot be understood just by knowing the meanings of words in the expression, such as *couch potato*) to determine the meaning of words and phrases.

Standard 2 – Reading Comprehension

4.2.1 Use the organization of informational text to strengthen comprehension.

Standard 3 – Literary Response and Analysis

4.3.3 Use knowledge of the situation, setting, and a character's traits and motivations to determine the causes for that character's actions.

Standard 4 – Writing Process

4.4.3 Write informational pieces with multiple paragraphs that: provide an introductory paragraph; establish and support a central idea with a topic sentence at or near the beginning of the first paragraph; include supporting paragraphs with simple facts, details, and explanations; present important idea or events in sequence or in chronological order; provide details and transitions to link paragraphs; conclude with a paragraph that summarizes the points, and use correct indention at the beginning of paragraphs.

Standard 5 – Writing Applications

4.5.6 Write for different purposes and to a specific audience or person.

Standard 6 – Written English Language Conventions

4.6.3 Create interesting sentences by using words that describe, explain, or provide additional details and connections, such as adjectives, adverbs, appositives, participial phrases, prepositional phrases, and conjunctions.

Standard 7 – Listening and Speaking

4.7.2 Summarize major ideas and supporting evidence presented in spoken presentations.

MSD Wayne Township, Indianapolis, IN
Safety Net Skills for
Language Arts Standards

GRADE 2

Standard 1 – Word Recognition, Fluency, and Vocabulary Development

2.1.1 Demonstrate awareness of the sounds that are made by different letters by distinguishing beginning, middle, and ending sounds in words; rhyming words; and clearly pronouncing blends and vowel sounds.

Standard 2 – Reading Comprehension

2.2.5 Restate facts and details in the text to clarify and organize ideas.

Standard 3 – Literary Response and Analysis

2.3.1 Compare plots, settings, or characters presented by different authors.

Standard 4 – Writing Process

2.4.2 Organize related ideas together to maintain a consistent focus.

Standard 5 – Writing Applications

2.5.2 Write a brief description of a familiar object, person, place, or event that: develops a main idea; uses detail to support the main idea.

Standard 6 – Written English Language Conventions

2.6.2 Distinguish between complete (*When Tom hit the ball, he was proud.*) and incomplete sentences (*When Tom hit the ball*).

Standard 7 – Listening and Speaking

2.7.8 Retell stories, including characters, setting, and plot.

Safety Net Skills for
Language Arts Standards

GRADE 11

Standard 1 – Word Recognition, Fluency, and Vocabulary Development

11.1.3 Analyze the meaning of analogies encountered, analyzing specific comparisons as well as relationships and inferences.

Standard 2 – Reading Comprehension

11.2.2 Analyze the way in which clarity of meaning is affected by the patterns of organization, repetition of the main ideas, organization of language, and word choice in the text.

Standard 3 – Literary Response and Analysis

11.3.2 Analyze the way in which the theme or meaning of a selection represents a view or comment on life, using textual evidence to support the claim.

Standard 4 – Writing Process

11.4.4 Structure ideas and arguments in a sustained and persuasive way and support them with precise and relevant examples.

Standard 5 – Writing Applications (Different Types of Writing and Their Characteristics)

11.5.3 Write reflective compositions that:

- explore the significance of personal experiences, events, conditions, or concerns by using rhetorical strategies, including narration, description, exposition, and persuasion.
- draw comparisons between specific incidents and broader themes that illustrate the writer's important beliefs or generalizations about life.
- maintain a balance in describing individual incidents and relate those incidents to more general and abstract ideas.

Standard 6 – Written English Language Conventions

11.6.1 Demonstrate control of grammar, diction, paragraph and sentence structure, and an understanding of English usage.

Standard 7 – Listening and Speaking

11.7.4 Use logical, ethical, and emotional appeals that enhance a specific tone and purpose.

Standard 7 – Listening and Speaking

MSD Wayne Township, Indianapolis, IN
Safety Net Skills for Language Arts Standards

GRADE 10

Standard 1 – Word Recognition, Fluency, and Vocabulary Development

10.1.2 Distinguish between what words mean literally and what they imply, and interpret what words imply.

Standard 2 – Reading Comprehension

10.2.4 Evaluate an author's argument or defense of a claim by examining the relationship between generalizations and evidence, the comprehensiveness of evidence, and the way in which the author's intent affects the structure and tone of the text.

Standard 3 – Literary Response and Analysis

10.3.2 Compare and contrast the presentation of a similar theme or topic across genres (different types of writing) to explain how the selection of genre shapes the theme or topic.

Standard 4 – Writing Process

10.4.5 Develop the main ideas within the body of the composition through supporting evidence, such as scenarios, commonly held beliefs, hypotheses, and definitions.

Standard 5 – Writing Applications

10.5.3 Write expository compositions, including analytical essays and research reports that:

gather evidence in support of a thesis (position on a topic), including information on all relevant perspectives.

communicate information and ideas from primary and secondary sources accurately and coherently.

make distinctions between the relative value and significance of specific data, facts, and ideas.

use a variety of reference sources, including word, pictorial, audio, and Internet sources to locate information in support of a topic.

include visual aids by using technology to organize and record information on charts, maps, and graphs.

anticipate and address readers' potential misunderstandings, biases, and expectations.

use technical terms and notations accurately.

Standard 6 – Written English Language Conventions

10.6.1 Identify and correctly use clauses, both main and subordinate; phrases, including gerund, infinitive, and participial; and the mechanics of punctuation, such as semicolons, colons, ellipses, and hyphens.

Standard 7 – Listening and Speaking

10.7.2 Choose appropriate techniques for developing the introduction and conclusion in a speech, including the use of literary quotations, anecdotes (stories about a specific event), or references to authoritative sources.

MSD Wayne Township, Indianapolis, IN
Safety Net Skills for Language Arts Standards

GRADE 12

Standard 1 – Word Recognition, Fluency, and Vocabulary Development

12.1.1 Understand unfamiliar words based on characters or themes in literature or on historical events.

Standard 2 – Reading Comprehension

12.2.5 Analyze an author's implicit and explicit assumptions and beliefs about a subject.

Standard 3 – Literary Response and Analysis

12.3.7 Analyze recognized works of world literature from a variety of authors that:

contrast the major literary forms, techniques, and characteristics from different major literary periods, such as Homeric Greece, Medieval, Romantic, Neoclassic, or the Modern Period.

relate literary works and authors to the major themes and issues of their literary period.

evaluate the influences (philosophical, political, religious, ethical, and social) of the historical period for a given novel that shaped the characters, plot, and setting.

Standard 4 – Writing Process

12.4.5 Enhance meaning by using rhetorical devices, including the extended use of parallelism, repetition, and analogy and the issuance of a call for action.

Standard 5 – Writing Applications

12.5.2 Write responses to literature that:

demonstrate a comprehensive understanding of the significant ideas in works or passages.

analyze the use of imagery, language, universal themes, and unique aspects of the text.

support important ideas and viewpoints through accurate and detailed references to the text and to other works.

demonstrate an understanding of the author's style and an appreciation of the effects created.

identify and assess the impact of perceived ambiguities, nuances, and complexities within the text.

Standard 6 – Written English Language Conventions

12.6.1 Demonstrate control of grammar, diction, paragraph and sentence structure, and an understanding of English usage.

Standard 7 – Listening and Speaking

12.7.18 Deliver oral responses to literature that:

demonstrate a comprehensive understanding of the significant ideas of literary works and make assertions about the text that are reasonable and supportable.

present an analysis of the imagery, language, universal themes, and unique aspects of the text through the use of speech strategies, including narration, description, persuasion, exposition, or a combination of those strategies.

support important ideas and viewpoints through specific references to the text and to other works.

demonstrate an awareness of the author's style and an appreciation of the effects created.

identify and assess the impact of ambiguities, nuances, and complexities within the text.

The Foreign Language "Safety Net"

Carole is also the district's Foreign Language Coordinator. After successfully developing the language arts "Safety Net," she repeated the process with Wayne Township's foreign language educators. Below is her commentary.

"Foreign language only involved grades 7 through 12 and its 'Safety Net' was decided in the same manner as we did language arts during the district's K-12 articulation day in the spring of 2001. We reviewed the foreign language state standards and indicators. Our discussions addressed each of the different languages we teach in the Township.

"Our eleven state standards for foreign language are excellent, and they focus on the following areas: **Communication**, **Cultures**, **Connections**, **Comparisons**, and **Communities**. Because these areas transcend all languages, our resulting foreign language 'Safety Net' is applicable to each one, and our foreign language teachers are all pleased with the process we followed."

I have included below Wayne Township's grades 7 through 12 foreign language "Safety Net," also reprinted with permission.

MSD Wayne Township, Indianapolis, IN
Safety Net Skills for
Foreign Language Standards

GRADES 7–12

Standard 1 – Students engage in conversations, provide and obtain information, express feelings and emotions, and exchange opinions.

    A.   Ask and answer simple questions about familiar topics orally and in writing.

Standard 2 – Students understand and interpret written and spoken language on a variety of topics.

    A.   Understand brief, written and oral materials on familiar topics.

Standard 3 – Students present information, concepts, and ideas to an audience of listeners or readers on a variety of topics.

    C. and E.

    Write a short paragraph of personal interest, and give short oral presentations on topics related to personal events and personal interests.

Standard 4 – Students demonstrate an understanding of the relationship between the practices and perspectives of the culture studied.

    C.   Identify similarities and differences of everyday life in the United States and the foreign culture.

Standard 5 – Students demonstrate an understanding of the relationship between the products and perspectives of the culture studied.

    C.   Identify major geographical features, historical events, and examples of artistic expression.

Standard 6 – Students reinforce and further their knowledge of other disciplines through the foreign language.

    A.   Identify and/or use information and skills from other disciplines in the foreign language classroom.

Standard 7 – Students acquire information and recognize the distinctive viewpoints that are only available through the foreign language.

    A.   Extract information from selected authentic sources.

Standard 8 - Students demonstrate understanding of the nature of language through comparisons of the language studied and their own.

> A. Identify basic grammatical structures of foreign language and compare them to their own.

Standard 9 – Students demonstrate understanding of the concept of culture through comparisons of the culture studied and their own.

> C. Recognize cross-cultural similarities and differences in practices, products, and perspectives.

Standard 10 –Students use the language both within and beyond the school setting.

> B. Identify occupations or professions that are enhanced by proficiency in another language.

Standard 11 - Students show evidence of becoming lifelong learners by using the language for personal enjoyment and enrichment.

> D. Experience samples of art, literature, music, etc., representative of the foreign culture.

Suggestions for Others

When I asked Carole if she had any advice she would like to give others who are beginning the Power Standards identification process, she replied, "I would recommend referencing the state's Testing Information Guide along with the state standards *before* trying to build consensus among teachers by asking them to prioritize the indicators based solely on personal opinion.

"Another important part of the process is to develop formative and summative assessments based on the 'Safety Net' indicators with teachers as the authors of those assessments. The assessments that are created, instructional strategies that are used, and the assessment information reported to parents should all relate directly back to the 'Safety Net.'

"The more teachers and principals you can involve in the process, the more powerful the results will be, and the more valued the final products will be. In large districts such as ours, this can be a logistical problem to solve, but one excellent way to achieve this is to utilize content area representatives at different buildings to build common language and communicate across grade levels."

If readers have more specific questions about the Wayne Township process in language arts or foreign language and wish further information, Carole Erlandson has graciously provided her contact information below.

> CAROLE ERLANDSON
> MSD Wayne Township
> Language Arts Coordinator, K-12
> 1220 South High School Road
> Indianapolis, IN 46241
> 317-243-5744
> 317-227-8648
> carole.erlandson@wayne.k12.in.us

K-12 Math "Safety Net"

Michele Walker, Math, Science, and Assessment Coordinator, K-12, explains in the following paragraphs the process she used with her committee members to create the Wayne Township K-12 math "Safety Net."

"The first step in the process of creating our mathematics 'Safety Net' was to discuss with math representatives from each of our ten elementary schools, along with all of the secondary math teachers, the philosophy and rationale for focusing our curriculum. We used Grant Wiggins and Jay McTighe's concentric circles to discuss curriculum that is 'nice to know, important to know, and essential to understanding' (2000). We also shared the triangle that Dr. Fenwick English illustrated when he performed a curriculum audit in our district a couple of years prior to that point in time. Dr. English spoke of the fact that the written curriculum, taught curriculum, and tested curriculum must all be aligned.

"After establishing this foundation with our teachers, we read Dr. Douglas Reeves' 'Safety Net' article [please see Appendix A] to further establish the need for a more focused curriculum. We emphasized the notion of 'working smarter, not harder.' Our state only has about six or seven mathematics standards at each grade, but there are an overwhelming number of indicators listed beneath those standards. Needless to say, the teachers were happy to learn about how to create a 'Safety Net' and implement the 'less is more' philosophy in their classrooms.

State Test Information

"After meeting as a large K-12 group to set the stage for our work, we divided the teachers into smaller groups by grade level. We provided data for the teachers in order to guide their selection of 'Safety Net' skills, including information about our state standardized test (ISTEP+), relative to the amount of emphasis placed on the different skill areas. By knowing how many points were possible in the category *Probability and Statistics* as compared to *Computation*, for example, the teachers were able to prioritize the standards and the indicators accordingly."

Vertical Articulation

Michele continues, "After examining the data, teachers were asked to create a first draft, listing the indicators they believed to be the ones that should comprise the 'Safety Net.' Then, the groups of teachers met with other grade levels to articulate across the grades. For instance, kindergarten teachers met with first grade teachers and sixth grade teachers met with seventh grade teachers. The purpose of this articulation was to ensure there were no gaps or overlaps in the 'Safety Net' curriculum.

The "Safety Net" Is Not All We Teach!

"We emphasized the notion that the 'Safety Net' would represent skills that *teachers would guarantee every student would master* prior to leaving their class to go on to the next grade. We also clearly stated that the 'Safety Net' curriculum is *not* all that we teach! We reminded teachers that there are still other indicators that are important to know, but that the 'Safety Net' means *all* students will *master* those particular skills in those particular grades.

Getting Feedback From All Teachers

"Elementary representatives went back to their schools and discussed the first draft with other teachers at their grade levels. Secondary teachers went back to school and reviewed with colleagues the first drafts for all math courses that they taught. On the district's articulation day, each teacher helped to create one grade's 'Safety Net.' During the next couple of months, all teachers placed tally marks beside the indicators they believed should be in the final version of the 'Safety Net.' The sheets with the tally marks were sent to my secretary, Getta McCann, in February, and she collated the information and prepared summary data regarding the first drafts."

Using State Test Data for Final Drafts

Michele continues, "The second district articulation day occurred in March. The grade levels met in grade spans of K-2, 3-4, 5-7, 8-9, and 9-12. (Our high school is comprised of grades 10-12, so ninth grade teachers were represented in two groups to ensure articulation between junior and senior high.) Teachers used summary data from their colleagues throughout the district, data that had been provided to them in the fall, and dialogue with representatives from adjacent grade levels to create a final draft of the 'Safety Net' during the March session.

"Since the selection of indicators for the 'Safety Net' was based on data, not all standards have the same number of indicators listed in the 'Safety Net'; in fact, it is possible for a grade level to have zero indicators listed for a particular standard. For example, in grade three, if the teachers noticed that the ISTEP+ test had very few points possible in *Geometry* and many points possible in several of the other standards, the teachers may have decided not to select any of the indicators in the *Geometry* area at all."

Distribution of the "Safety Net"

Michele concludes, "During the spring and summer months, my secretary typed the 'Safety Net' skills and printed individual color copies on cardstock. Then we sent the copies to a professional print shop to be laminated with a hard film. When school started in the fall, teachers received a laminated card (8½ x 11) containing a copy of the 'Safety Net' for their grade level on the front and the previous grade level on the back. Teachers also received a non-laminated copy of the 'Safety Net' skills for the grade level above their own. They were thrilled to receive the end products in time to better focus their mathematics instruction for the new school year!"

Included below are three randomly selected grade-level examples from the K-12 mathematics "Safety Net," reprinted with permission. To view the entire K-12 math "Safety Net," please visit the Wayne Township website address included at the end of this chapter.

GRADE 1

Standard 1 – Number Sense
Students understand symbols, objects, and pictures used to represent numbers up to 100 and show an understanding of fractions.

  1.1.1   Count, read, and write whole numbers up to 100.

  1.1.10   Represent, compare, and interpret data using pictures and picture graphs.

Standard 2 – Computation
Students demonstrate the meaning of addition and subtraction and use these operations to solve problems.

  1.2.1   Show the meaning of addition (putting together, increasing) using objects.

  1.2.2   Show the meaning of subtraction (taking away, comparing, finding the difference) using objects.

  1.2.4   Demonstrate mastery of the addition facts (for totals up to 20) and the corresponding subtraction facts.

Standard 3 – Algebra and Functions
Students use number sentences with symbols +, - , and = to solve problems.

  1.3.1   Write and solve number sentences from problem situations involving addition and subtraction.

Standard 4 – Geometry
Students identify common geometric shapes, classify them by common attributes, and describe their relative position or their location in space.

  1.4.1   Identify, describe, compare, sort, and draw triangles, rectangles, squares, and circles.

  1.4.6   Arrange and describe objects in space by position and direction: near, far, under, over, up, down, behind, in front of, next to, to the left or right of.

Standard 5 – Measurement
Students learn how to measure length, as well as how to compare, order, and describe other kinds of measurement.

  1.5.6   Tell time to the nearest half-hour and relate time to events (before/after, shorter/longer).

  1.5.7   Identify and give the values of pennies, nickels, and dimes.

Standard 6 – Problem Solving
Students make decisions about how to set up a problem. Students solve problems and justify their reasoning.

  1.6.1   Choose the approach, materials, and strategies to use in solving problems.

  1.6.3   Explain the reasoning used and justify the procedures selected in solving a problem.

GRADE 5

Standard 1 – Number Sense
Students compute with whole numbers, decimals, and fractions and understand the relationship among decimals, fractions, and percents. They understand the relative magnitudes of numbers. They understand prime and composite numbers.

5.1.1   Convert between numbers in words and numbers in figures, for numbers up to millions and decimals to thousandths.

5.1.3   Arrange in numerical order and compare whole numbers or decimals to two decimal places by using the symbols for less than (<), equals (=), and greater than (>).

Standard 2 – Computation
Students solve problems involving multiplication and division of whole numbers and solve problems involving addition, subtraction, and simple multiplication and division of fractions and decimals.

5.2.1   Solve problems involving multiplication and division of any whole numbers.

5.2.2   Add and subtract fractions (including mixed numbers) with different denominators.

Standard 3 – Algebra and Functions
Students use variables in simple expressions, compute the value of an expression for specific values of the variable, and plot and interpret the results. They use two-dimensional coordinate grids to represent points and graph lines.

5.3.7   Use information taken from a graph or equation to answer questions about a problem situation.

Standard 4 – Geometry
Students identify, describe, and classify the properties of plane and solid geometric shapes and the relationships between them.

5.4.1   Measure, identify, and draw angles, perpendicular and parallel lines, rectangles, triangles, and circles by using appropriate tools (e.g., ruler, compass, protractor, appropriate technology, media tools).

5.4.4   Identify, describe, draw, and classify polygons, such as pentagons and hexagons.

GRADE 5 (continued)

Standard 5 – Measurement

Students understand and compute the areas and volumes of simple objects, as well as measuring weight, temperature, time, and money.

5.5.2   Solve problems involving perimeters and areas of rectangles, triangles, parallelograms, and trapezoids, using appropriate units.

5.5.7   Add and subtract with money in decimal notation.

Standard 6 – Data Analysis and Probability

Students collect, display, analyze, compare, and interpret data sets. They use the results of probability experiments to predict future events.

5.6.1   Explain which types of displays are appropriate for various sets of data.

5.6.2   Find the mean, median, mode, and range of a set of data and describe what each does, and does not, tell about the data set.

Standard 7 – Problem Solving

Students make decisions about how to approach problems and communicate their ideas. Students use strategies, skills, and concepts in finding and communicating solutions to problems. Students determine when a solution is complete and reasonable and move beyond a particular problem by generalizing to other situations.

5.7.2   Decide when and how to break a problem into simpler parts.

5.7.3   Apply strategies and results from simpler problems to more complex problems.

5.7.4   Express the solution clearly and logically by using the appropriate mathematical terms and notation. Support solutions with evidence in both verbal and symbolic work.

Safety Net Skills for
Mathematics Standards

ALGEBRA I

Standard 1 – Operations with Real Numbers

Students simplify and compare expressions. They use rational exponents and simplify square roots.

A1.1.2   Simplify square roots using factors.

A1.1.3   Understand and use the distributive, associative, and commutative properties.

Standard 2 – Linear Equations ad Inequalities

Students solve linear equations and inequalities in one variable. They solve word problems that involve linear equations, inequalities, or formulas.

A1.2.1   Solve linear equations.

A1.2.6   Solve word problems that involve linear equations, formulas, and inequalities.

Standard 3 – Relations and Functions

Students sketch and interpret graphs representing given situations. They understand the concept of a function and analyze the graphs of functions.

A1.3.1   Sketch a reasonable graph for a given relationship.

A1.3.2   Interpret a graph representing a given situation.

Standard 4 – Graphing Linear Equations and Inequalities

Students graph linear equations and inequalities in two variables. They write equations of lines and find and use the slope and y-intercept of lines. They use linear equations to model real data.

A1.4.1   Graph a linear equation.

A1.4.2   Find the slope, x-intercept and y-intercept of a line given its graph, its equation, or two points on the line.

A1.4.3   Write the equation of a line in slope-intercept form. Understand how the slope and y-intercept of the graph are related to the equation.

ALGEBRA I (continued)

Standard 5 – Pairs of Linear Equations and Inequalities

Students solve pairs of linear equations using graphs and using algebra. They solve pairs of linear inequalities using graphs. They solve word problems involving pairs of linear equations.

> A1.5.1   Use a graph to estimate the solution of a pair of linear equations in two variables.
>
> A1.5.3   Understand and use the substitution method to solve a pair of linear equations in two variables.
>
> A1.5.5   Understand and use multiplication with the addition or subtraction method to solve a pair of linear equations in two variables.

Standard 6 – Polynomials

Students add, subtract, multiply, and divide polynomials. They factor quadratics.

> A1.6.1   Add and subtract polynomials.
>
> A1.6.4   Multiply polynomials.
>
> A1.6.6   Find a common monomial factor in a polynomial.

Standard 7 – Algebraic Fractions

Students simplify algebraic ratios and solve algebraic proportions.

> A1.7.2   Solve algebraic proportions.

Standard 8 – Quadratic, Cubic, and Radical Equations

Students graph and solve quadratic and radical equations. They graph cubic equations.

> A1.8.2   Solve quadratic equations by factoring.
>
> A1.8.6   Solve quadratic equations by using the quadratic formula.

Science "Safety Net" Grades 7-12

Michele Walker describes below the process she used to identify the district's science "Safety Net" for grades 7 through 12. (The K-6 component was created before she assumed the role of Science Coordinator.)

Secondary Science

"I followed virtually the same process in science as the one we followed in mathematics. Teachers met in small groups by grade level in seventh and eighth grade and by course in grades 9-12. After discussing with them the rationale for identifying a 'Safety Net' for their science standards and indicators, we provided data to guide the teachers in their selection of the 'Safety Net' skills. As we did with the mathematics group, we included information about our state standardized test (ISTEP +) in terms of the amount of emphasis placed on the different skill areas. We referenced cross-curricular programs implemented in science classes, such as *Writing Across the Curriculum* and *Mathematics Across the Curriculum* (in-house programs developed by and implemented in Wayne Township). Knowing how many points were possible in each of the English/ language arts and mathematics categories on ISTEP + helped the teachers prioritize the science standards and indicators.

"Once the first drafts of the 7-12 science 'Safety Net' were completed, groups of secondary science teachers met to articulate the selected indicators across the grades. For example, seventh grade teachers met with eighth grade teachers and chemistry teachers met with physics teachers. The purpose of this articulation was to ensure there were no gaps or overlaps in the 'Safety Net' curriculum.

"As we did in mathematics, we emphasized that the 'Safety Net' would represent skills that teachers would *guarantee every student would master* prior to leaving their class to go on to the next grade, that the 'Safety Net' curriculum is *not* all that we teach, and reminded the science teachers that there are still other indicators that are important to know, even though they exist outside the 'Safety Net.'

"We then collected feedback about our initial draft of the 'Safety Net' from secondary science teachers for all science courses they taught. We used that feedback to make any needed revisions, they were typed by my secretary, Kim Albedyll, and the final 'Safety Net' cards were then laminated and distributed to all. This process absolutely works!"

Included below are two randomly selected grade-level examples from the grades 7-12 science "Safety Net," also reprinted with permission. To view the entire secondary science "Safety Net," please visit the Wayne Township website address included at the end of this chapter.

GRADE 7

Standard 1 – The Nature of Science and Technology

Students further their scientific understanding of the natural world through investigations, experiences, and readings. They design solutions to practical problems by using a variety of scientific methodologies.

7.1.1   Recognize and explain that when similar investigations give different results, the scientific challenge is to judge whether the differences are trivial or significant, which often takes further studies to decide.

7.1.3   Explain why it is important in science to keep honest, clear, and accurate records.

Standard 2 – Scientific Thinking

Students use instruments and tools to measure, calculate, and organize data. They frame arguments in quantitative terms when possible. They question claims and understand that findings may be interpreted in more than one acceptable way.

7.2.1   Find what percentage one number is of another and figure any percentage of any number.

7.2.7   Incorporate charts, circle, bar, and line graphs, diagrams, scatter plots, and symbols into writing, such as lab or research reports, to serve as evidence for claims and/or conclusions.

Standard 3 – The Physical Setting

Students collect and organize data to identify relationships between physical objects, events, and processes. They use logical reasoning to question their own ideas as new information challenges their conceptions of the natural world.

7.3.1   Recognize and explain that the sun is a medium-sized star located near the edge of a disk-shaped galaxy of stars and that the universe contains many billions of galaxies, with each galaxy containing many billions of stars.

7.3.4   Explain how heat flow and movement of material within the Earth causes earthquakes and volcanic eruptions and creates mountains and ocean basins.

7.3.12   Investigate how the temperature and acidity of a solution influences reaction rates, such as those resulting in food spoilage.

7.3.17   Investigate how an unbalanced force acting on an object changes it speed or path of motion, or both, and know that if the force always acts towards the same center as the object moves, the object's path may curve into an orbit around the center.

Standard 4 – The Living Environment

Students begin to trace the flow of matter and energy through ecosystems. They recognize the fundamental difference between plants and animals and understand its basis at the cellular level. Students distinguish species, particularly through an examination of internal structures and functions. They use microscopes to observe cells and recognize that cells function in similar ways in all organisms.

7.4.4   Explain how cells continually divide to make more cells for growth and repair and that various organs and tissues function to serve the needs of cells for food, air, and waste removal.

7.4.5   Explain how the basic functions of organisms, such as extracting energy from food and getting rid of wastes, are carried out within the cell and understand that the way in which cells function is similar in all organisms.

7.4.6   Explain how food provides the fuel and the building material necessary for all organisms.

Standard 6 – Historical Perspectives

Students gain understanding of how the scientific enterprise operates through examples of historical events. Through the study of these events, they understand that new ideas are limited by the context in which they are conceived, that the ideas are often rejected by the scientific establishment, that the ideas sometimes spring from unexpected findings, and that the ideas grow or transform slowly through the contributions of many different investigators.

7.6.4   Understand and explain that changes in health practices have resulted from the acceptance of the germ theory of disease. Realize that before germ theory, illness was treated by appeals to supernatural powers or by trying to adjust body fluids through induced vomiting, bleeding, or purging. Understand that the modern approach emphasizes sanitation, the safe handling of food and water, the pasteurization of milk, quarantine, and aseptic surgical techniques to keep germs out of the body; vaccinations to strengthen the body's immune system against subsequent infection by the same kind of microorganisms; and antibiotics and other chemicals and processes to destroy microorganisms.

Safety Net Skills for
Earth and Space Science Standards

Standard 1 – Principles of Earth and Space Science

Students investigate, through laboratory and fieldwork, the universe, the Earth, and the processes that shape the Earth. They understand that the Earth operates as a collection of interconnected systems that may be changing or may be in equilibrium. Students connect the concepts of energy, matter, conservation, and gravitation to the Earth, solar system, and universe. Students utilize knowledge of the materials and processes of the Earth, planets, and starts in the context of the scales of time and size.

ES.1.5   Understand and explain the relationship between planetary systems, stars, multiple-star systems, star clusters, galaxies, and galactic groups in the universe.

ES.1.10   Recognize and explain that the earth sciences address planet-wide interacting systems, including the oceans, the air, the solid Earth, and life on Earth, as well as interactions with the solar system.

ES.1.15   Understand and describe the origin, life cycle, behavior, and prediction of weather systems.

ES.1.23   Explain motions, transformations, and locations of materials in the Earth's lithosphere and interior (e.g., describe the movement of the plates that make up the crust of the Earth and the resulting formation of earthquakes, volcanoes, trenches, and mountains).

ES.1.28   Discuss geologic evidence, including fossils and radioactive dating, in relation to the Earth's past.

Contact Information

Like Carole Erlandson, Michele has also graciously agreed to share her contact information if readers need more specific information as to how the K-12 math and 7-12 science "Safety Nets" were developed.

> Michele Walker
> Math, Science, and Assessment Coordinator, K-12
> 1220 South High School Road
> Indianapolis, IN 46234
> 317-243-8251
> Fax: 317-243-5744
> michele.walker@wayne.k12.in.us

K-12 Social Studies "Safety Net"

Dr. Janet Boyle, assistant principal of Ben Davis High School and Social Studies and Physical Education Coordinator, followed the same process Carole Erlandson developed for identifying the "Safety Nets" in both language arts and foreign language. Her following commentary describes the process she and her committee members used for K-12 social studies and K-6 physical education:

"During the 2001-02 school year, I met with my entire K-12 social studies group to determine our 'Safety Net' indicators. In attendance were about 60 elementary teachers representing each grade from each of our ten elementary schools and approximately 40 secondary teachers in all grades, seven through twelve, from our three junior high schools and Ben Davis High.

"There are only five Indiana social studies standards in grades K-8. In Wayne Township, there are seven high school history courses that address anywhere from 5 to 11 standards in each one. The secondary social studies representatives faced a greater challenge than the elementary in attempting to prioritize large numbers of indicators under each major standard. For instance, in U.S. history, a few of the standards have over 20 indicators each.

"We used the same criteria Larry Ainsworth and Doug Reeves suggest for the selection process: what students need for success in school (leverage; readiness for next levels of learning), in life (endurance), and on the state test. For most standards, the teachers selected the one indicator that was their top choice as being the most important for students to learn. For those standards with an especially large number of indicators, the teachers selected their top two to four indicators rather than just one. In making these determinations, the teachers relied on their experience as well as professional discussion and negotiation to determine which indicators represented broader knowledge and skills or those that encompassed several objectives.

"Indiana does not presently administer a state assessment in social studies, but eventually social studies will be assessed in grades five, seven, and nine. When the state does begin its testing program for social studies, I anticipate that teachers will want to revisit their 'Safety Net' choices to determine needed revisions."

Department Chair Commentary on the Process

Paul Buck, history chair at Ben Davis High School, shared with me the process he successfully used with his department.

"We divided up according to the courses we were currently teaching. At that time we did not have a state history test to consider when selecting our Power Standards. So I asked the history teachers within each course to rely on their experience and knowledge of the subject matter to individually select the three standards within that course that they thought were essential for student understanding and success. We then tallied the results. Those standards with the most tallies became our Power Standards.

"It wasn't a perfect process, and not everyone agreed with the final list, of course, but at least we had general agreement among us that these were the ones to really teach for depth of student understanding. I made it clear that having our Power Standards did not preclude teachers from emphasizing other standards in their instruction that they personally considered important for students to learn. It just gave us a common basis of agreement about which standards were critical for students to know in order for them to have a strong foundation of historical knowledge."

Compromise, Timeframes, and Curriculum Writing

Janet Boyle continues, "Social studies is so content-heavy, it was tough to decide which era under a standard to emphasize the most. So we had to compromise and prioritize several eras. For instance, some teachers wanted to spend nine weeks on the Civil War. Our new standards make it clear that this is an important unit of study, but not to the exclusion of other standards. So teachers discussed timeframes for teaching the year's content, and this yielded compromises on length of time spent on certain units.

"I was amazed by an unexpected side benefit to our extensive work in identifying the 'Safety Net' indicators through this process. During the summer of 2002, our social studies curriculum writing was finished in just two half-days! Even though we were utilizing a new curriculum-writing software program, I attribute our speed in accomplishing the task to our teachers' deep familiarity with the standards and indicators."

I have included below three randomly selected examples of Wayne Township's K-12 social studies "Safety Net," reprinted with permission. To view the entire K-12 social studies "Safety Net," please visit the Wayne Township website address included at the end of this chapter.

KINDERGARTEN

STANDARD	INDICATOR #	INDICATOR NARRATIVE
1. **History** – Students examine the connections of their own environment with the past, begin to distinguish between events and people of the past and the present, and use a sense of time in classroom planning and participation	K.1.4	Identify and order events that take place in a sequence. *Examples: Identify events in the school day as first, next, last; sequence the day's activities in the classroom; place events, such as birthdays, in order; use a calendar to identify national holidays and historical events.*
2. **Civics and Government** – Students learn that they are citizens of their school, community, and country, identify symbols of the state and nation, understand examples of responsible citizenship, follow school rules, and know why rules are needed for order and safety.	K.2.2	Give examples of rules in the classroom and school, and provide reasons for the specific rules.
3. **Geography** – Students learn that maps and globes are different ways of representing the earth's surface and begin to explore the geographic characteristics of their homes, school, and community.	K.3.1	Use words related to location, direction, and distance, including *here/there, over/under, left/right, up/down.*
4. **Economics** – Students explain how people do different jobs and work to meet basic economic wants.	K.4.1	Explain that people work to earn money to buy the things they want.
5. **Individuals, Society, and Culture** – Students identify themselves as individuals who interact with other individuals and groups, including the family, school, and community; and identify ways that people, who are similar and different, make up the community.	K.5.2	Identify individuals who are important in students' lives, such as parents, grandparents, guardians, and teachers, and give examples of how families cooperate and work together.

STANDARD	INDICATOR #	INDICATOR NARRATIVE
1. **History** – Students will trace the historical periods, places, people, events, and movements that have led to the development of Indiana as a state.	4.1.3	Explain the importance of the Revolutionary War and other key events and people that influenced Indiana's development. *Examples: George Rogers Clark and the Fall of Fort Sackville (1779), U.S. land treaties with Indians, Chief Little Turtle, Tecumseh, Tenskwatawa (the Prophet), William Henry Harrison, the Battle of Tippecanoe (1811).*
2. **Civics and Government** – Students will describe the components and characteristics of Indiana's constitutional form of government; explain citizenship rights and responsibilities; investigate civic and political issues and problems; use inquiry and communication skills to report findings in charts, graphs, written, and verbal forms; and demonstrate responsible citizenship by exercising civic virtues and participation skills.	4.2.3.	Identify and explain the major responsibilities of the legislative, executive and judicial branches of state government as written in the Indiana Constitution.
3. **Geography** – Students will explain how earth/sun relationships influence the climate of Indiana; identify the components of earth's physical systems; describe the major physical and cultural characteristics of Indiana; give examples of how the interaction of people with their environment has changed over time and continues to change; and identify regions of Indiana.	4.3.1	Use latitude* and longitude* to locate places in Indiana and other parts of the world. * Latitude: Imaginary lines that circle the globe from east to west. The equator is the line of latitude that divides the globe into two equal hemispheres. * Longitude: Imaginary lines that circle the globe from north to south and pass through the poles.
4. **Economics** – Students will study and compare the characteristics of Indiana's changing economy in the past and present.	4.4.1	Give examples of the kinds of goods* and services* produced in Indiana in different historical periods. * Goods: Tangible objects, such as food, that can satisfy people's wants. * Services: *Actions that someone does for you, such as disposal of trash*
5. **Individuals, Society, and Culture** – Students will examine the interaction between individual and group behavior in state and community life; analyze the roles and relationships of diverse groups of people contributing to Indiana's cultural heritage; and describe the impacts of science, technology, and the arts on Indiana's culture.	4.5.3	Define the term cultural group*, and give examples of the challenges faced by diverse cultural groups in Indiana history. * Cultural group: A group of people who share common language, religion, customs *Examples: Quakers faced religious and social differences. Recent Asian and Hispanic immigrants face the challenge of adapting to a new language and culture.*

GRADE 9

STANDARD #1 – **BEGINNING OF HUMAN SOCIETY** – Students will examine the lives of the hunting and gathering people of the ancient world during the beginnings of human society.

> 1st INDICATOR – **WH.1.1** – Trace the approximate chronology and territorial range of early human communities, and analyze the processes that led to their development.

> 2nd INDICATOR – **WH.1.2** – Analyze and compare how peoples of West Africa, Europe, Southeast Asia, East Asia, and the Americas domesticated food plants and developed agricultural communities in response to local needs and conditions.

STANDARD #2 – **EARLY CIVILIZATIONS 4000 TO 1000 BCE.** - Students will examine the characteristics of early civilizations including those of Egypt, Mesopotamia, the Indus River Valley, and China from 4000 to 1000 BCE.

> 1st INDICATOR – **WH.2.2** – Compare causes and conditions by which civilizations developed in Egypt, Southwest Asia and the Eastern Mediterranean region, India, and China, and explain why the emergence of these civilizations was a decisive transformation in human history.

> 2nd INDICATOR – **WH.2.4** – Construct a time line of main events on the origin and early development of civilizations in Mesopotamia, Egypt, the Indus Valley, and China.

STANDARD #3 – **CLASSICAL CIVILIZATIONS OF GREECE AND ROME, 2000 BCE TO 500 CE** - Students will examine the antecedents, origins, development, and achievements of the classical civilizations of Greece and Rome from 2000 BCE to 500 CE

> a. Greek

> > 1st INDICATOR – **WH.3.2** – Describe the institutions and traditions of the Greek city-based republics, their influence on the lives of citizens and other residents, and their impact on the development of democratic and republican forms of government.

> > 2nd INDICATORS –

> > > **WH.3.4** – Analyze the major events of the wars between Persians and the Greeks, reasons why the Persians failed to conquer the Greeks, and consequences of the wars for Greek civilization.

> > > **WH.3.5** – Compare and contrast the daily life, social hierarchy, culture, and institutions of Athens and Sparta; describe the rivalry between Athens and Sparta, and explain the causes and consequences of the Peloponnesian War.

> b. Roman

> > 1st INDICATOR – **WH.3.8** – Describe Roman republican government and society, and trace the changes that culminated in the end of the republic and the beginning of the Roman Empire.

> > 2nd INDICATORS –

> > > **WH.3.9** – Describe Roman achievement in law and technology and explain their impact on various peoples and places in subsequent periods of world history.

> > > **WH.3.12** – Explain the causes, conditions, and consequences of the decline and fall of the western part of the Roman Empire.

Safety Net Skills for Social Studies Standards
GRADE 9 (continued)

STANDARD #4 – MAJOR CIVILIZATIONS, STATES, AND EMPIRES IN ASIA, AFRICA, AND THE AMERICAS, 1000 BCE TO 1500 CE – Students will trace the development of major civilizations, states, and empires in different regions of Asia, Africa, and The Americas from 1000 BCE to 1500 CE.

    a. Asia

        1st INDICATOR – **WH.4.2** – Use various primary and secondary sources to examine, interpret, and compare the main ideas of Hinduism and Buddhism, and explain their influence on civilization in India.

        2nd INDICATORS –

            WH.4.4 – Trace the development and major achievements of Chinese civilization during various key dynasties, such as the Zhou, Qin, Han, Tang, and Song.

            WH.4.5 – Describe the life of Confucius; compare the fundamental teachings of Confucianism and Taoism, and explain the influence of these ideas on Chinese civilization.

    b. Africa

        1st INDICATOR – **WH.4.11** – Describe the rise and fall of the ancient east African kingdoms of Kush and Axum and the development of Ethiopia.

        2nd INDICATOR – **WH.4.14** – Explain the origins and development of the slave trade in Africa and its connections to Arabic peoples of North Africa and Southwest Asia and to Western European peoples.

    c. Pre-Columbian Americas

        1st INDICATOR – **WH.4.16** – Compare and contrast the Maya, Aztec, and Inca civilizations in terms of their arts, religion, sciences, economy, social hierarchy, government, armed forces, and imperial expansion.

STANDARD #5 – MEDIEVAL EUROPE AND RISE OF CIVILIZATION 500 TO 1500 – Students will examine the political, economic, social and cultural development of Europe, which influenced the rise of Western Civilization from 500 to 1500.

    1st INDICATORS –

        WH.5.1 – Describe the impact on Western Europe of the collapse of the Roman Empire.

        WH.5.2 – Describe the importance of Christian monasteries and convents as centers of education, political power, economic productivity, and commercial life, and describe their roles in spreading the Christian religion and civilization throughout Western and Central Europe.

    2nd INDICATORS –

        WH.5.4 – Describe the rise and achievements of Charlemagne and the Empire of the Franks, and explain how the idea of Christendom influenced the development of cultural unity in Europe.

        WH.5.5 – Define feudalism and the manorial system, and explain their impact upon European civilization.

STANDARD #6 – RENAISSANCE AND REFORMATION IN EUROPE AND THE DEVELOPMENT OF WESTERN CIVILIZATION, 1250 TO 1650 – Students will examine the antecedents, events, outcomes, and legacy for Western Civilization of the Renaissance and Reformation from 1250 to 1650.

    1st INDICATOR – **WH.6.2** – Describe the main themes and achievements of the Renaissance, including its impact on science, technology and the arts. *Example: Recognize and explain the importance of the artists of the southern and northern Renaissance, such as Michelangelo, Leonardo da Vinci, Brueghel.*

    2nd INDICATORS –

        WH.6.3 – Analyze the social and cultural impact of the invention of the printing press upon the Renaissance and the Protestant Reformation.

        WH.6.5 – Trace the spread of Protestantism across Europe and the reactions of the Catholic Church, and explain the influence of the Reformation on the development of Western Civilization.

STANDARD #7 – WORLDWIDE EXPLORATION, CONQUEST, AND COLONIZATION, 1450 TO 1750 – Students will examine the causes, events, and consequences of European worldwide exploration, conquest, and colonization from 1450 to 1750.

> 1st INDICATOR – **WH.7.1** – Explain the causes and conditions of worldwide voyages of exploration and discovery by expeditions from Portugal, Spain, France, England, and the Netherlands.

STANDARD #8 – **SCIENTIFIC, POLITICAL, AND INDUSTRIAL REVOLUTIONS, 1500 TO 1900** – Students will examine the causes, events, and global consequences of the scientific, political, and industrial revolutions that originated in Western Europe and profoundly influenced the world from 1500 to 1900.

> 1st INDICATOR – **WH.8.3** – Analyze the impact of science upon technology, government, economy, and society in Europe, and explain the global importance of the Scientific Revolution.

> 2nd INDICATORS –

>> **WH.8.5** – Explain the concept of "the Enlightenment" in European history, and describe its impact upon political thought and government in Europe, North America, and other regions of the world.

>> **WH.8.6** – Compare and contrast the causes and events of the American and French Revolutions of the late eighteenth century and their consequences for the growth of liberty, equality, and democracy in Europe, North America, and other parts of the world.

STANDARD #9 – **GLOBAL IMPERIALISM, 1750 TO 1900** – Students will examine the origins, major events, and consequences of worldwide imperialism from 1750 to 1900.

> 1st INDICATOR – **WH.9.2** – Define and explain the causes, main events, and global consequences of nineteenth-century imperialism.

> 2nd INDICATOR – **WH.9.6** – Analyze the causes and consequences of Russian imperialism on central Asia and Siberia.

STANDARD #10 – **ERA OF GLOBAL CONFLICTS, CHALLENGES, CONTROVERSIES, AND CHANGES, 1900 TO 2001** – Students will analyze and explain twentieth century trends and events of global significance, such as world wars, international controversies and challenges, and cross-cultural changes that have connected once separated regions into an incipient global community.

> 1st INDICATOR – **WH.10.1** – Trace and explain the antecedents, causes, major events, and global consequences of World War I.

> 2nd INDICATORS –

>> **WH.10.4** – Trace and explain the antecedents, causes, major events, and global consequences of World War II, including the Holocaust.

>> **WH.10.6** – Trace and explain the antecedents, causes, major events, and global consequences of the Cold War.

STANDARD #11 – **HISTORICAL RESEARCH** – Students will conduct historical research that includes forming research questions, developing a thesis, investigating a variety of primary and secondary sources and presenting their findings with documentation.

> 1st INDICATOR – **WH.11.1** – Locate and analyze primary and secondary sources presenting differing perspectives on events and issues of the past. *Example: Primary and secondary sources should include a balance of electronic and print sources, such as autobiographies, diaries, maps, photographs, letters, newspapers, and government documents.*

> 2nd INDICATOR – **WH.11.2** – Locate and use sources found at local and state libraries, archival collections, museums, historic sites, and electronic sites.

K-6 Physical Education "Safety Net"

Janet summarizes below the procedure she followed to develop the K-6 "Safety Net" for physical education.

"There are only ten elementary P.E. teachers in the district, one for each elementary school. So instead of lots of paper and pencil 'voting,' we were able to accomplish the preliminary selection of the 'Safety Net' indicators through one e-mail communication with input from all ten of them. We then met together as a group, and they made their final decisions.

"They zeroed right in on which indicators they thought deserved the most emphasis. They determined these indicators mostly through their own judgment using the same three selection criteria all the other content areas have used.

"Keep in mind, these are veteran P.E. teachers who are very strong advocates for their standards. They each have only 30 to 40 minutes per grade level per week to teach each group of students. Because of their limited time, they know exactly which standards are foundational for subsequent teaching. This knowledge helped them narrow their focus quickly.

"In the primary grades, the teachers identified the indicators that develop large motor skills and coordination. As the teachers continue to build a foundation of skills in their students, they then add to and expand their expectations for what the students can do.

"Once the final list of 'Safety Net' indicators for K-6 was completed, I followed Carole's example again and laminated a desk copy for each grade so that each P.E. teacher would have every grade's prioritized indicators to reference as s/he planned lessons and activities. I did take the process one step further by creating a wall poster of all K-6 identified 'Safety Net' indicators that I duplicated for display in each elementary school's gym.

"I agree with Carole Erlandson that the *process* is the beauty of this endeavor—more so than the final product. The level of professional conversation increased greatly as teachers in both social studies and physical education worked through this entire process."

I have included below a reduced copy of Wayne Township's K-6 physical education "Safety Net" wall poster, reprinted with permission. To view each individual grade's P.E. "Safety Net," please visit the Wayne Township website address included at the end of this chapter.

STANDARD	KINDERGARTEN	GRADE ONE	GRADE TWO	GRADE THREE	GRADE FOUR	GRADE FIVE	GRADE SIX
Demonstrate competency in many movement forms and proficiency in a few movement forms	K.1.1 – Perform locomotor (traveling actions) and non-locomotor (movement in place) skills at a beginning level. *Example: Walk, run, hop, jump, skip, leap, gallop, slide, swing, sway, bend, stretch, and twist with variation in speed, direction, force, shape, and level in general and personal space.* K.1.2 – Perform stability (balance) skills alone and/or with a partner. *Example: Transfer weight so as to perform rocking, rolling, flight, and step-like actions. Balance on a beam or perform simple stunts and tumbling skills like the stork stand or log roll.* K.1.3 – Manipulate objects (throw, catch, strike, swing, push, pull) at a basic level. *Example: Throws an object with an overhand-underhand motion using various speeds, levels, and directions. Jumps rope.* K.1.4 – Perform basic rhythmic skills alone and with a partner. *Example: Perform exercises or simple dances to music or to teacher/student produced rhythmical sounds.*	1.1.1 – Demonstrate the ability to perform locomotor (walk, run, traveling actions) and non-locomotor (movement in place) skills upon teacher request. *Example: Respond to imagery, such as waves on the seashore by using various non-locomotor movements like twisting, bending, or swaying.* 1.1.2 – Perform basic balance skills a lone with a partner, or on various apparatus. *Example: Perform simple stunts like the stork stand or back-to-back partner sit.* 1.1.3 – Manipulate a variety of objects (throw, catch, strike, kick) while moving or standing still, using variations in force/effort. *Example: Attempt throwing at various speeds, distances, and at targets. Catches medium sized objects in activities like Hot Potato.* 1.1.4 – Perform basic rhythmic skills alone, with a partner, or within a group. *Example: Move creatively to even/uneven rhythms or to a variety of musical rhythms and styles using simple dance steps.*	2.1.1 – Demonstrate the ability to perform locomotor (traveling actions) and non-locomotor (movement in place) skills proficiently. *Example: Run, walk, and skip to music. When music stops they swing, sway, bend, reach without moving from their spot.* 2.1.2 – Demonstrate the ability to perform stability (balance) skills alone/or with a partner. *Example: Walk across a balance beam suspended 6 inches from the floor or any other object.* 2.1.3 – Demonstrate the ability to manipulate (throw, catch, strike, swing, push, pull) objects. *Example: Jump a self-twirled rope.* 2.1.4 – Demonstrate the ability to perform basic rhythmic skills alone and with a partner. *Example: Participate in jumping rope to music, coordinating the speed of the jump with the tempo (rate or speed) of the music.*	3.1.1 – Demonstrate movement skills with many variations. *Example: Explore variations of throwing a ball (overhand, underhand, sidearm, one hand, two hands).* 3.1.2. – Combine different movement skills to form more complex skills. *Example: Dribble a soccer ball while running at different speeds and using the inside and outside of the feet.* 3.1.3 – Utilize implements (bat, ball, racquet) combined with motor skills (movement skills) to perform specific skills. *Example: Using a size-appropriate bat, strike a ball that is thrown by a partner.* 3.1.4 – Demonstrate motor skill (movement skills) patterns following various rhythms. *Example: Bounce, pass, and catch a ball to the rhythm of music.*	4.1.1 – Demonstrate mature movement patterns in locomotor (traveling actions), non-locomotor (movement in place), and manipulative (throw, catch, strike, swing, push, pull) skills. *Example: Catch, throw, kick, and run using mature form.* 4.1.2 – Demonstrate combinations of motor (movement) skills for specific sports. *Example: Catch, dribble, and pass a basketball to a moving partner.* 4.1.3 – Demonstrate complex patterns of movement in applied settings. *Example: Design and demonstrate part of a rhythmical movement program.*	5.1.1 – Demonstrate the ability to integrate locomotor (traveling action), non-locomotor (movement in place), and stability (balance) movements in more complex skills. *Example: Demonstrate mature motor (movement) patterns in increasingly complex environments (e.g., obstacle courses).* 5.1.2 – Demonstrate the ability to manipulate (throw, catch, strike, swing, push, pull) objects with the skills necessary to participate in games and lead-up activities. *Example: Engage in simple games requiring manipulative skills.* 5.1.3 – Demonstrate the ability to perform more complex rhythmic skills alone and with a partner. *Example: Perform rhythmic body movements and communicate ideas and feelings with and without music.*	6.1.1 – Demonstrate mature forms in locomotor (traveling actions), non-locomotor (movement in place), and manipulative (throw, catch, strike, swing, push, pull) skills. *Example: Dribble a basketball around stationary objects using both right and left hands.* 6.1.2 – Demonstrate basic competency in more complex motor (movement) skills related to specific sports activities. *Example: Develop a 60-second dance program using combinations of locomotor (traveling actions) and non-locomotor (movement in place) skills with changes of direction, pace, and level.*
Applies movement concepts and principles to the learning and development of motor (movement) skills	K.2.1 – Identify and uses a variety of relationships with objects.	1.2.2 – Identify the characteristics of mature locomotor (traveling actions), non-locomotor (movement in place), and manipulative (throw, catch, strike, swing, push, pull) skills. *Example: Circle pictures or state key indicators of correct form for the overhand throw.*	2.2.4 – Understand and demonstrate strategies for simple games and activities. *Example: Plan strategies to use in playing a simple game of Capture the Flag.*	3.2.3 – Identify the use of various amounts of force to propel (move) objects varying distances. *Example: Kick a ball using light force, medium force, and hard force to see what distance the ball achieves at each force level.*	4.2.2 – Apply the concept of practice to improve skills in appropriate settings. *Example: Using chest pass with a basketball, pass ball to a target successfully 10 times.*	5.2.1 – Identify ways that movement concepts can be used to refine movement skills. *Example: Understand that practice improves performance.*	6.2.2 – Explain how practicing movement skills improves performance. *Example: Maintain a log of practice attempts for throwing a softball at a target, comparing differences in successful throws from first attempts to last attempts.*
Exhibits a physically active lifestyle	K.3.1 – Participate in moderate to vigorous physical activity during and after school. *Example: Participate fully in physical education class activities, and in unstructured play with friends, family, or through organized movement experiences for young children.*	I.3.1 – Participate in lifetime activities during physical education and recess. *Example: Participate in a twenty-minute fitness walk (fast walk) during physical education class.*	2.3.3 – Define and identify activities associated with health-related (healthy lifestyle) physical activity. *Example: Engage in activities and behaviors that demonstrate health concepts.*	3.3.1 – Participate actively in all physical education classes. *Example: Enter game situations or movement practice without prompting.*	4.3.1 – Describe the physical, motional and psychological benefits of participation in health-related (healthy lifestyle) activities. *Example: List the benefits that result from participation in health-related activities.*	5.3.1 – Participate in health enhancing physical activity. *Example: Establish physical activity goals.*	6.3.2 – Participate in activities, outside of school, that are health enhancing and can be continued throughout a lifetime. *Example: Report in portfolio that they played a round of golf with a parent on a Saturday.*
Achieves and maintains a health-enhancing level of physical fitness	K.4.1 – Set goals for an age appropriate level of health-related fitness (healthy lifestyle). *Example: Students determine that one of his/her fitness goals is to be able to run 10 laps around the gymnasium without walking.*	1.4.1 – Demonstrate how increasing the intensity of activity will increase their heart rate. *Example: Participate in locomotor (traveling actions) activities with the teacher controlling the intensity of the activity with commands—walk, skip, jog, run, etc. They cease activity after each level and feel the beating of their hearts. They are asked to describe the difference in the heart beats between each level.*	2.4.3 – Understand the components (parts) of health-related (healthy lifestyle) fitness. *Example: Describe the components of health-related fitness as being strong hearts, strong muscles, lean bodies, and good range of motion.*	3.4.1 – Participate in self assessment and formal fitness assessments. *Example: Assess self using the Fitnessgram (a fitness test) assessment.*	4.4.1 – Participate in self-assessment for physical fitness and meets the standards for that particular age test for their appropriate age group. *Example: Take and meet the age appropriate standards for the Fitness gram (a fitness test) assessment of health-related (healthy lifestyle) fitness.*	5.4.1 – Achieve a reasonable level in all components of health-related (healthy lifestyle) fitness. *Example: Using a pre-test and post-test, demonstrate how to set personal fitness goals.*	6.4.2 – Develop individual goals for each of the health-related (healthy lifestyle) fitness components. *Example: Set a goal to successfully perform 10 pull-ups before Thanksgiving.*

STANDARD	KINDERGARTEN	GRADE ONE	GRADE TWO	GRADE THREE	GRADE FOUR	GRADE FIVE	GRADE SIX
Demonstrate responsible personal and social behavior in physical activity settings	K.5.1 - Demonstrate an understanding of rules, regulations, and safety practices. *Example: Follow and is able to verbalize rules in physical education class and on the playground. Use appropriate safety equipment and follow safe practices in class and on the playground. Participate in activities without intentionally colliding into other students or objects.*	1.5.2 - Demonstrate a willingness to work with other students toward a common goal. *Example: Participate with a partner or team in a game situation requiring problem solving skills.*	2.5.2 - Work cooperatively with other students; exhibit individual, partner, small, and large group socialization skills regardless of personal differences. *Example: Engage easily in low organization (few rules and low level skills) games requiring cooperative play.*	3.5.1 - Demonstrate good sportsmanship in and out of class activities. *Example: Accept losses in competition without whining or placing blame.*	4.5.2 - Follow rules and safe practices in all class activities without being reminded. *Example: Stop activity immediately upon signal from teacher.*	5.5.3 - Distinguish between compliance and noncompliance with game rules and fair play. *Example: Demonstrate positive sportsmanship.*	6.5.1 - Participate in cooperative activities in both a leadership and a follower role. *Example: Choose partners for a cooperative activity who they feel can work efficiently and successfully together to reach a group goal.*
Demonstrate understanding and respect for differences among people in physical activity settings	K.6.1 - Demonstrate positive attitudes toward self and others through physical activity. *Example: Play cooperatively with others.*	1.6.1 - Demonstrate a willingness to help a fellow student who has difficulty completing a skill. *Example: Offer to demonstrate a skill to a student who is unable to do the skill.*	2.6.4 - Display cooperation with others when resolving conflicts. *Example: Demonstrate positive sportsmanship, encourage playmates, and do not dispute officials' calls.*	3.6.2 - Accept and give constructive (helpful) criticism. *Example: Gives verbal assistance to a partner to help him/her successfully bat a ball.*	4.6.3 - Recognize the limitations of persons with disabilities and understand the adaptations (changes) they make when participating in physical activity. *Example: While participating blindfolded, students work with partners who lead them through an obstacle course.*	5.6.4 - Resolve conflict in socially accepted ways. *Example: Demonstrate positive sportsmanship.*	6.6.2 - Display an appreciation of the accomplishments of both greater and less skilled individuals in group or team activities. *Example: Participate in a follow-up discussion after a cooperative game, noting the positive contributions of each group member.*
Understands that physical activity provides the opportunity for enjoyment, challenge, self-expression, and social interaction	K.7.1 - Exhibit self-confidence and enjoyment when participating in movement experiences. *Example: Attempt new activities after being introduced to the activities.*	1.7.2 - Set short term goals that will require practice and work to achieve. *Example: Participate in self-testing activities.*	2.7.3 - Engage in and enjoy independent and interaction (with others) physical activity. *Example: Choose to practice a new skill alone first and later with a partner.*	3.7.2 - Enjoy participation in partner and team physical activities. *Example: Move with a partner over an obstacle course, helping each other as needed.*	4.7.3 - Participate in new and challenging physical activities. *Example: Traverse the low elements on a traverse rock climbing wall in physical education class.*	5.7.3 - Engage in and enjoys independent and interactive physical activity. *Example: Incorporate physical skills during leisure time activities.*	6.7.3 - Identify the social, emotional and physical benefits of participation in physical activities. *Example: Write a theme about how it feels to successfully master a new physical skill.*

Contact Information

Janet Boyle has also graciously agreed to share her contact information if readers need more specific information as to how the K-12 social studies and K-6 physical education "Safety Nets" were developed.

Dr. Janet Boyle
Assistant Principal for Curriculum & Professional Development
Ben Davis High School
1200 N. Girls School Road
Indianapolis, IN 46214
317-227-4564
fax: 317-243-5506
janet.boyle@wayne.k12.in.us

Wayne Township's Website

I have personally shared the 'Safety Net' examples from Wayne Township with educators all over the United States. Without exception, there has been unanimous praise for the work their district has accomplished. I have received more requests for copies of their 'Safety Nets' in the different content areas than I can possibly count, and Wayne Township has continually shared their work with school systems nationwide. Even though standards and indicators vary in language and format from state to state, Wayne Township's vertical alignment model is what educators want to reference as they develop their own set of state-specific Power Standards.

You may wish to visit Wayne Township's district website at < www.wayne.k12.in.us > to view their "Safety Net" Power Standards for language arts, mathematics, science, social studies, foreign language, and physical education. Simply go to their above home page web address, then click on "Curriculum," click next on "Standards", and you will see their Power Standards.

Due to the ongoing requests for copies of their "Safety Nets," Wayne Township has now made them available to download from their website "for free." I wish to formally thank Wayne Township's educators and administrators for their generosity in sharing this valuable work with us all.

In Conclusion

Wayne Township takes its rightful place among our nation's exemplary school systems for sustaining a vision of excellence through commonsense practices designed to improve the quality of instruction and the corresponding achievement of its students. Dr. Terry Thompson, superintendent, has year after year upheld a steady focus on Power Standards, performance assessments aligned to the Power Standards, writing across the curriculum, and a comprehensive accountability system to measure and continually improve results in student learning.

To summarize the importance of systematically prioritizing the standards with the involvement of all district educators, I believe the words of Assistant Superintendent Dr. Karen Gould say it best:

> "Power Standards have done what we expected them to do—focus our work so we can better prepare our students and raise achievement levels."

CHAPTER FIVE

Caldwell, Idaho

How It All Began

Caldwell is an Idaho community of about 25,000 residents located in the greater Boise valley approximately 25 miles from Boise. Nan Woodson, professional development associate with the Center for Performance Assessment, worked closely with Rick Miller, superintendent of Caldwell School District #132, and his curriculum staff to identify their Power Standards. Following are Nan's and Rick's combined commentary describing how this process was initiated and completed in Caldwell.

Rick began, "My standards planning committee and I had spent months searching out districts that were realizing degrees of success in implementing standards and achieving results. During my research, I noticed that when other superintendents and national presenters spoke of standards, assessment, curriculum, and accountability, the names Dr. Douglas Reeves and the Center for Performance Assessment continually came up. I called the Center, and we began what would become a long-term relationship."

Nan said, "It was decided that Caldwell's first priority was to better utilize test data to improve student performance on state assessments. I presented the Center's one-day *Data-Driven Decision Making* seminar four times over four days. Principals attended the first two days in order to learn the process that they would later lead their faculties through. They then returned on the second two days with their teacher-leader teams so they could assist them in learning the process and discuss the application of the information within the specific context of their individual schools.

"In December of 2001, I presented a brief overview of the Center's *Making Standards Work* seminar to about 30 curriculum teacher-leaders. Once they saw the Wayne Township Power Standards examples in the supporting documents, they wanted to get started on their own versions immediately. This group was hungry for change! These teacher-leaders recognized that the Power Standards would provide the key to better organization, less stress, clearer direction, and the bottom line: increased student achievement on their state assessments.

"The standards planning committee, under the leadership of Rick and his colleague Margo Healy, Language Arts Coordinator and Director of Professional Development, decided to convene the four major K-12 content committees in math, social studies, science, and language arts. Rick and Margo provided time and generous stipends for these educators to examine the current Idaho standards and the published information explaining the Northwest Assessment, Idaho's new state assessment published by the

Northwest Evaluation Association (www.nwea.org). This information provided descriptions of what students needed to know and be able to do at each grade level in order to demonstrate proficiency. With these documents at their disposal, the four content area groups got to work identifying their Power Standards."

The Standards Planning Committee

Rick added, "Caldwell advocates and promotes teacher leadership. Because Power Standards are a teacher leadership and classroom issue, it was critical to the success of Power Standards in Caldwell to involve and empower the professional educators in our schools and classrooms. The standards planning committee, which designed and planned all of the Power Standards activities and implementation plans, is made up primarily of classroom teachers, with limited administrative representation. Each curriculum committee is also comprised of classroom teachers from each school site and is led by a teacher/curriculum coordinator for that subject area."

Caldwell's Plan of Action

Nan continued, "The plan of action was to allocate five full days, immediately after school was out in June, for the identification of the Power Standards in each of the four major content areas. The work was to be done by the teacher-led curriculum committees and their teacher/curriculum coordinator in each of the four disciplines. Workrooms were provided at the high school for the four teachers (one representing each curriculum area) from each building who had agreed to be part of this process. A teacher/curriculum coordinator would work with each of the four content committees to keep the process focused and moving forward.

"To build knowledge and confidence in their ability to carry out their facilitation role, I conducted a separate training session with these four teacher leaders from each site, using the Power Standards material in Part One of the *Making Standards Work* workshop manual to thoroughly familiarize them with the process."

Rick interjected, "As part of this plan, it was also decided that in order to create a level of buy-in from all Caldwell schools and teachers, each of the four curriculum committees would include teachers that were selected at each school site by that local staff. This allowed each school to have four teachers who were involved in the curriculum and had specific curriculum and standards expertise. In addition to creating a strong bond between the four teacher-leaders at each site, it would enable the four teacher-leaders to present a 'united front' when presenting the Power Standards to their building colleagues in the fall."

Nan continued, "Principals were kept abreast of all plans and communications between central office and the teacher-leaders. In addition, they were requested to attend the first morning of the five-day Power Standards identification sessions for a keynote address by Rick Miller and an explanation of the work about to take place. Principals were also requested to attend the afternoon of the fifth day to meet with their four teacher representatives in order to plan how to share this information with their entire staffs upon their return in the fall.

"The agenda for these building meetings would include:

- An explanation of Power Standards

- A summary of how Power Standards were identified

- A review by teachers of the initial drafts

- The opportunity for teachers to provide feedback for later revisions using a standard form to expedite the collection of reactions from all the schools."

The Five-Day Agenda with Commentary

The following five-day agenda with commentary summarizes the Power Standards identification process Caldwell educators followed under Nan's direction.

Day 1: Organize, Provide Materials, and Begin Process

- Present Power Standards, Part 1 of *Making Standards Work*

- Assign participants to classrooms for specific content area work

    Materials and equipment available in work rooms: laptop computers; overhead projectors; copies of "The Learning Continuum" (Northwest Evaluation Association assessment information guides); markers; chart paper; curriculum books; teacher guides; other documents such as PSSM (Principles and Standards for School Mathematics); National Council of Teachers of English (NCTE) documents; National Science Standards; National Council of Social Studies (NCSS) documents; etc.

- Begin identification of Power Standards for assigned content area

Nan said, "My job during the committee work times each day was to visit the rooms in which groups were working to observe progress, answer questions, provide support, and offer feedback as needed. Questions for me were recorded on a piece of chart paper so I could specifically address them during my visits.

"As the first draft of each grade's Power Standards was copied onto large chart paper, it was posted on the wall so that every member of the committee could see the flow of standards from grade to grade. This focus on vertical alignment remained uppermost in everyone's mind."

Day 2: Develop Rubric for Selection Criteria; Continue Process

- Meet with all participants to create a rubric for Power Standards selection criteria

- Review work completed and make revisions according to rubric

- Continue Power Standards identification using rubric's selection criteria

Nan explains, "The participants really were able to create a powerful rubric to guide the continuation of their process since they had spent the first day making preliminary decisions about which standards and indicators should be designated 'power.' They used a four-point scale and focused on the proficient category of '3' to determine whether or not their already identified Power Standards met all the proficient criteria. Those criteria included:

- Enduring

- Foundational

- Provides leverage

- Rigorous

- Clear

- Aligned with NWEA and district assessments

- Measurable

- Appropriate for grade level."

Day 3: Share-outs by Content Area Groups; Continue Process

- Each content area committee briefly shares with the large group two or three identified Power Standards that "passed" the proficient criteria test

- Continue working in content area groups

Day 4: Continue Process

- Check in briefly with all groups

- Continue working in content area groups

Day 5: Presentations by Content Areas; Plan for Presentation to Faculties

- Meet all together to review objectives and agenda for this last day

- Complete work in content area groups during the morning

- Each content area group presents their Power Standards in the afternoon

- Principal-teacher teams meet to plan how to introduce process to entire faculties

Nan says, "By the end of the fifth day, only the social studies group had completed the entire Power Standards identification process, but the science group was almost complete. Math and language arts still had more to do, so Margo Healy announced that there was enough money in her budget for those groups to meet the following week to complete and refine their work.

"Rick Miller promised to disperse copies of their identified Power Standards to all the sites as soon as the content area groups submitted electronic versions. When school begins in the fall of 2002, teachers at each building will receive the Power Standards information and be given the opportunity to provide feedback on the drafts. This feedback will be used to create second drafts. In this way, every teacher in the district will have ownership in the process."

In conclusion, Rick describes how that information was eventually shared.

"On the first day back to school in September, 2002, the entire district staff reviewed the efforts of the teacher committees from the summer and were given the written Power Standards for each grade and core content area. School principals and their four teacher-leaders led their site faculties in a further review of the Power Standards and the process used to identify them."

Published Caldwell Power Standards

Caldwell has since published their Power Standards for grades K-8 in two formats: colorful tri-fold brochures for parents and handsome wall posters for displaying in classrooms. On the front of each brochure and poster appear the specific grade in bold print along with a descriptor that reads, "What your child will LEARN and must be able to DEMONSTRATE COMPETENCY IN, by the END OF THE SCHOOL YEAR." Inside each brochure and on each poster are the identified Power Standards for that grade in the content areas of language arts, mathematics, science, and social studies. The Idaho State Standards Implementation Fund has generously provided the funding for the publication of Caldwell's Power Standards brochures and posters.

Included below are representative grade-level examples of Caldwell's Power Standards, reprinted with permission.

Caldwell Schools
3rd Grade Power Standards

LANGUAGE ARTS

Word Recognition, Fluency, and Vocabulary Development
- Decode and encode words using phonics code and grade level sight words
- Read grade level connected text with fluency of 120 wpm

Reading Comprehension
- Recognize and interpret significant detail in text to comprehend meaning

Literary Response and Analysis
- Create detailed graphic organizers including elements of setting, character, plot and resolution

Writing Process
- Create paragraphs with topic sentences and simple supporting details

Writing Applications
- Given a prompt, write a narrative utilizing adjectives and descriptive phrases to enhance writing

Written English Language Conventions
- Write complete sentences of statements, command, question, or exclamation with correct capitalization and punctuation
- Recognize correct application of basic spelling rules including: change y to i and add ending and drop final "e", and add -ing, -ed, -ous

Listening and Speaking
- Ask and answer questions completely and appropriately

MATHEMATICS

Number Sense and Numeration
- Read, write, order, and compare whole numbers to 100,000
- Identify and interpret place value in whole numbers to 100,000
- Recognize and represent commonly used fractions (halves, thirds, fourths, and eighths)

Computation
- Add and subtract whole numbers up to 1,000 with and without regrouping
- Represent the concept of multiplication as repeated addition

Geometry

- Identify and represent right angles, line segments, intersecting and parallel lines

Measurement

- Measure line segments to the nearest half-inch and centimeter
- Determine, by counting, the value of a collection of coins and bills up to $10.00
- Compute the perimeter of rectangle using inches and centimeters
- Represent and tell time in five-minute intervals

Problem Solving

- Analyze and solve problems by identifying relationships, telling relevant from irrelevant information, sequencing and prioritizing information, and observing patterns
- Round to the nearest hundred to estimate solutions to problems
- Apply the four-step method to the strategies: *Use or make a table;* Guess and check

Algebra and Functions

- Define and apply the mathematical properties of addition
- Represent mathematical relationships (>, <, =) of quantities in the form of a numeric expression or equation

Statistic and Probability

- Record observations and interpret information from tables, charts, and graphs to explain and justify conclusions
- Predict, perform, and record results of probability experiments

SCIENCE

Life Science

- Compare plant life cycles by germinating seeds and growing plants hydroponically
- Relate animal structures/functions and behaviors to their environments
- Record similarities and differences of organisms
- Create and compare habitats to observe the basic needs of a living organism

Physical Science

- Observe magnetic interactions and sort objects based on whether they are affected by a magnet
- Measure and record the force of attraction between magnets at a distance
- Identify materials that are electrical conductors and insulators

Earth Science

- Identify the properties of water (solid, liquid gas), interactions between water and other earth materials and how humans use water
- Observe, record, and explain what happens to water as it is heated, cooled, frozen, evaporated, condensed, and allowed to interact with soil and gravel
- * *Note: The following standards have not been "unwrapped" as they are included in the above standards.*

Inquiry

- Plan and conduct simple investigations
- Employ tools to gather data, display data in simple tables, and use the data to
- Communicate the results of scientific investigations to others through oral and written language

Science-Technology- Society

- Use equipment, including computer software, to collect, measure, analyze, and summarize data; to prepare reports; and to communicate
- Illustrate how technology (how people use knowledge, tools, and systems) is used in the community to make life better

Themes and Patterns

- Observe, record, and compare changes and patterns in organisms and materials (i.e. life cycles, phase changes)
- Construct and use models to illustrate interactions and changes (water and soil, heat and water, model of a flashlight)

Interpersonal Skills

- Abide by school rules
- Demonstrate proper scientific safety procedures
- Work and discuss in collaborative groups to problem solve

SOCIAL STUDIES

Government

- Identify and explain the basic functions of local government.
- Compare the basic roles of presidents, governors, and mayors.

Geography

- Locate on a map: waterways, landforms, cities, states, and national boundaries using standard map symbols.

History

- Explain your own personal history as a part of the community.

Culture

- Compare different culture groups within the community, including their different foods, clothing styles, and traditions.

Economics

- Explain the difference between goods and services.

Citizenship

- List qualities of a good leader.
- Explain why communities have laws, and why following them is important.

Skills

- Create a school map and legend, including cardinal directions.

Caldwell Schools
6th Grade Power Standards

LANGUAGE ARTS

Word Recognition, Fluency, and Vocabulary Development
- In narrative text, apply knowledge of text structure to determine the meaning of unfamiliar words and phrases
- Read grade level text correctly with a fluency rate of 145 words per minute

Reading Comprehension
- Demonstrate comprehension of grade level text by using text structures; summarizing, comparing and contrasting, and classifying

Literary Response and Analysis
- Identify and analyze features of themes conveyed through characters, actions, and images

Writing Process
- Write informational pieces with multiple purposes that:
  - Engage the reader
  - State a clear purpose
  - Develop a topic with supporting details and precise language
  - Conclude with detail summary linked to the purpose of the composition

Writing Applications
- Write essays utilizing text structure (descriptions, explanations, compare/contrast and time order to clearly state the thesis (position of topic) or purpose

Written English Language Conventions
- Write simple and compound sentences with correct pronouns (reflexive, nominative, possessive, objective).
- In written work apply basic spelling patterns to correctly spell ance, -ence, -ei/ie, -ary, -ery, and plural forms

Listening and Speaking
- Plan and deliver oral presentations that effectively incorporate the following transitions, organization, support of main ideas, examples, response to questions and feedback, visual aids and appropriate technology

MATHEMATICS

Number Sense and Numeration

- Order and graph integers
- Identify decimals to the hundred-thousandths using word form and standard form
- Identify the least common denominator for two or more fractions

Computation

- Add and subtract mixed numbers with unlike denominators
- Add and subtract decimals to ten-thousandths
- Multiply and divide fractions
- Solve proportions

Geometry

- Classify regular polygons by sides and angles
- Classify angle pairs (supplementary and complementary)

Measurement

- Identify and apply the relationships within the metric and customary systems
- Measure angles with a protractor
- Calculate the area of triangles and other irregular figures (based on polygons)

Problem Solving

- Apply the four-step method to solve problems
- Choose and use an appropriate problem solving strategy
- Estimate to determine if solutions to word problems are reasonable

Algebra and Functions

- State a rule to explain a number pattern and apply a rule to complete a function table
- Simplify numeric expressions by applying mathematical properties of rational numbers

Statistics and Probability

- Compute and compare the mean, median, and mode of a set of data

SCIENCE

Physical Science

- Use words, diagrams, and models to explain how forces influence the motion of an object
- Use models and experimental evidence to illustrate how heat as a form of energy affects matter and is transferred from place to place
- Relate the properties of waves to the characteristics and use of sound and light in our world
- Conduct experiments to demonstrate how electricity produces magnetism and how magnetism produces electricity
- Analyze the characteristic properties and the changes in the properties of matter

  Note: The following standards have not been "unwrapped" as they are included in the above standards.

Inquiry

- Obtain scientific information from a variety of sources
- Collect and record data using line graphs, charts, and tables

Science-Technology-Society

- Use laboratory equipment to correctly measure mass, volume, length, and temperature in metric units with appropriate precision

Themes and Patterns

- Use physical and mental models to illustrate the composition of matter and the interactions between matter and energy

Interpersonal Skills

- Abide by CSD Middle School Science Safety contract by demonstrating techniques and behaviors appropriate for each activity
- Record observations, data and results in a laboratory notebook
- Work productively as a member of a group to accomplish task

SOCIAL STUDIES

Government
- Explain the evolution of city, state into empire
- Show the significance of the first uniform code of law and social justice.

Geography
- Identify geographical features: cape, delta, flood plain
- Use latitude and longitude to locate places on a map
- Spell correctly and locate on a map the seven continents and four oceans.

History
- Differentiate social classes and their influence on society.

Culture
- Explain the contributions to our world today made by ancient civilizations: Mesopotamia, Egypt, Greece, Rome, the Mayans, Incas, Aztecs; the people of the Huang He and Indus river valleys.
- Compare the characteristics of Hinduism, Judaism, and Christianity.
- Differentiate between monotheism and polytheism.

Economics
- Show the relationship between the development of trade and specialization.

Citizenship
- Justify using majority rule to protect minority rights.
- Justify how education is a foundation for civilization.
- Show the importance of compromise and negotiation to resolve conflicts.

Skills
- Create a timeline using a ruler
- Place locations, scale, and geographical features on a map
- Create graphs and charts

Caldwell Schools Website

Caldwell's Power Standards for grades K-8 have also been posted on the district's website for easy access by all members of the Caldwell community. When I contacted Rick for permission to reprint selected grade level examples of Power Standards, he kindly offered the Caldwell website address as well so that readers can view Caldwell's K-8 Power Standards in their entirety.

The Caldwell School District website address is < www.caldwellschools.org >. On the left side of their home page is a menu that includes Power Standards. Click on the button that corresponds to the grade desired and it will link to the Power Standards for that grade in the four content areas of language arts, math, science, and social studies.

Conclusion and Contact Information

Nan concludes, "This was an extremely rewarding process to facilitate and observe. At the end of the last day, participants received a very nice certificate of appreciation for their contribution to this important project. I was presented with a certificate that stated, 'I survived teaching the Caldwell School System how to identify the Power Standards!'"

For more information on how Nan Woodson and Rick Miller guided Caldwell School District through this process, please contact Nan at the following address:

Nan Woodson
Center for Performance Assessment
1660 S. Albion St. Suite 1110
Denver, CO 80222
800-844-6599 ext. 515
nwoodson@makingstandardswork.com

CHAPTER SIX

Palm Springs, California

Background

Palm Springs Unified School District (PSUSD) is a large K-12 district in the southern California desert approximately 100 miles east of Los Angeles.

In October of 2000, Mr. Frank Tinney, Director of Standards, Assessment and Accountability for PSUSD, other members of the Educational Services staff, and all Palm Springs principals attended the first of a two-part presentation by Dr. Douglas Reeves sponsored by the Riverside County Office of Education.

In April of 2001, Eileen Allison, professional development associate with the Center for Performance Assessment, was invited to meet with the Palm Springs Educational Services department and representatives of teachers and administrators from across the district.

Frank states, "The focus of this first gathering was Curriculum Council training, and the outcome was the design format for developing a scope and sequence that was standards-based. The decision was made to create a framework for each core subject area that began with the grade 12 standards and 'flowed backward' to pre-Kindergarten. We wanted this document to include all of the California academic standards and highlight those standards that would, at a later stage, be identified as our Power Standards."

Eileen worked closely with Frank Tinney and Lorraine Becker, Assistant Superintendent for Educational Services, to establish an organizational plan for the next step, one that would involve all principals and educators in this process.

Principal-Curriculum Team Partnerships

Eileen explains, "In the summer of 2001, I worked with a core curriculum team representing math, language arts, science, and social studies, and a number of principals. Each principal was paired with a curriculum committee member. The plan was for these partnerships to co-facilitate the Power Standards identification process with every school faculty. Because of the district's strong commitment to involve *everyone*, the Palm Springs central office administrators taught the Power Standards identification process to all the principals in the district who were not members of this curriculum committee.

"After the process was introduced in all the schools by the principal-curriculum committee member partnerships, each building submitted drafts of Power Standards in the language arts domain of writing. The input from each faculty was collected and used by the language arts subgroup of the original curriculum committee.

"A standards-based scope and sequence was produced that listed all the standards for a particular content area, arranged from grade 12 down to pre-school. The Power Standards that represented the consensus of the committee appeared in the documents in bold, italicized fonts."

Frank adds, "All of the California standards with our Power Standards highlighted for each grade (elementary) and course (secondary) were published in handbook form with accompanying classroom posters and distributed to teachers in the fall of 2001."

Comprehensive Standards-based Reform Efforts

Identification of the Power Standards was the critical first step in implementing the district's vision for standards-based reform. Related professional development within the district focused on the design of standards-based performance assessments, standards-based grading and reporting systems, an accountability system that included data-driven decision making, and how to transition from a traditional to a standards-based school system.

Frank describes in the following paragraphs what has resulted since the identification of the Palm Springs Power Standards:

"After facilitating the identification of our Power Standards, Eileen helped in the development of standards-based performance assessments, course descriptions for the core subjects in grades 12 to 6, and end-of-course assessments. Throughout the 2001-02 school year, Eileen and Bette Frazier (professional development associate with the Center for Performance Assessment) facilitated the design of end-of-course assessments for ninth and tenth grade English, Algebra, and Geometry (see the "Educators Guide" document below).

"In February of 2002, the staff development coordinator and I attended the certification training for *Making Standards Work* with Larry Ainsworth, and that 3-day workshop became a prerequisite for future end-of-course assessment design teams.

"In June of 2002, I conducted the *Making Standards Work* training with a group that included all of the teachers who would later work with Eileen, Bette, and Michelle LePatner (professional development associate with the Center for Performance Assessment) over the summer to design end-of-course assessments for Physical Science, Biology, and World History. I also worked with the music educators to identify our Power Standards for Music.

"On August 29, 2002, Dr. Douglas Reeves delivered the keynote address for our entire teaching and administrative staff to kick off the new school year!"

Factors Contributing to Palm Springs' Success

Eileen Allison summarizes the factors she believes were critical in Palm Springs' efforts to realize the comprehensive reform efforts that began with their identification of Power Standards only a year before.

- "I believe the reason that Palm Springs has achieved such tremendous progress in such a short amount of time is due to the incredible ***positive leadership*** provided by Frank Tinney and Lorraine Becker. Frank and Lorraine possess commitment, honesty, patience, a sense of humor, and the perseverance to follow through. They listen to good ideas, and once they believe something has merit for improving student achievement, they tenaciously support it.

- "Another key factor is the ***administrative commitment to providing as much professional development time*** as possible to support the highest levels of learning. Of course it feels that there is never enough time, but Palm Springs has gone the extra mile in this regard. They have paid teachers additional stipends to work during the summer and on weekends.

- "District leadership holds to ***a vision that goes beyond one piece of the puzzle***. Their commitment to achievement for all students and development of the Power Standards provided the unifying elements to realize that vision. From the very beginning, they knew they would need to attend simultaneously to several initiatives that collectively contributed to an increase in student achievement. I believe they were able to do this because of Frank's coordination and organizational skills.

- Palm Springs is ***committed to building capacity in all district personnel***. Every professional development service provided by the Center for Performance Assessment has included a "trainer of trainers" component so that their own personnel can, in complete confidence, continue supporting these practices in the future."

Eileen concludes, "An important goal of mine as a Center consultant was to help Palm Springs develop a common set of definitions, ideas, and processes with regard to their use of standards. Frank Tinney has supported this by creating practices that place the Power Standards front and center within the district. At this point, Power Standards are on the tip of everyone's tongue!"

Palm Springs Unified School District Website

For readers who would like to view the Palm Springs Power Standards, please visit their district website at < www.psusd.k12.ca.us >. Once the home page appears, click on "Power Standards" on the menu bar in the upper right hand corner. This will link to the Power Standards page.

The Palm Springs Educator's Guide and Contact Information

For the publication of this book, Mr. Tinney generously provided the *Educator's Guide to the Palm Springs Unified School District End-of-Course Assessments*, an introductory document to the collection of end-of-course assessments written by Eileen Allison and Palm Springs educators. If you would like more information about this document and the assessments that were created, please refer to his contact information below.

> Mr. Frank Tinney
> Director of Standards, Assessment and Accountability
> Palm Springs Unified School District
> Palm Springs, California
> 760-416-6079 (District)
> ftinney@psusd.k12.ca.us

Readers may also wish to contact Eileen Allison for further information relating to any of the processes described in this chapter. Her contact information is as follows:

> Eileen Allison
> Center for Performance Assessment
> 1660 S. Albion St. Suite 1110
> Denver, CO 80222
> 800-844-6599 ext. 517
> eallison@makingstandardswork.com

Educator's Guide to the
Palm Springs Unified School District
End-of-Course Assessments

2002 Edition

TABLE OF CONTENTS

INTRODUCTION

This Educator's Guide is written for teachers in the Palm Springs Unified School District who are using end-of-course assessments designed by teachers in the Palm Springs School District and the Center for Performance Assessment. The purpose of this guide is to describe the end-of-course assessments and provide administration procedures. These assessments have two parts to them. There is a multiple-choice section composed of 30 problems and there is a constructed response section composed of 10 tasks.

Every test item evaluates student proficiency in the *"Power Standards"* identified by the Palm Springs Unified School District.

BACKGROUND

The Palm Springs Unified School District has embarked on a comprehensive process to align curriculum, instruction, assessment, evaluation and accountability activities to rigorous and essential academic standards.

Committees involving teachers and administrators representing all schools, grade levels and departments have been working together since the spring of 2001 to create and revise curriculum, assessments and progress reporting processes. Some of the projects include:

- An aligned scope and sequence of standards from grades Pre-K to 12
- The identification of "Power Standards"
- The creation of performance assessments to measure student proficiency in selected "Power Standards"
- Creation of standards-based course descriptions, developed around the "Power Standards"
- Research and review of standards-based report cards
- The creation of end-of-course assessments for several secondary classes

QUESTIONS AND ANSWERS ABOUT THE END-OF-COURSE ASSESSMENTS

Q. What is the purpose of using end-of-course assessments?

A. Because teachers are expected to demonstrate that their students are proficient in the academic standards for their course, it is important that the students are evaluated using a number of assessment tools. The end-of-course assessments provide a summative indicator of students' proficiency in the "Power Standards" identified for the course. End-of-course assessments are *one* way for students to demonstrate proficiency on one or more "Power Standards" that were taught during the year. Other assessments that can be used in conjunction with the end-of-course assessments might include ongoing performance assessments, achievement tests, reports, special projects, teacher-created tests, chapter tests from books, demonstrations, and all the many ways that teachers already evaluate students. The end-of-course assessments are *one* piece of evidence about student achievement, not *the* piece of evidence of student achievement.

Q. Who designed the materials?

A. The writers of the assessment materials are Palm Springs Unified School District (PSUSD) teachers with expertise and experience in the subject area and grade level assessed. What makes these end-of-course assessments unique to the Palm Springs School District is the collaboration between the teachers who wrote the assessments and the Center for Performance Assessment. Each assessment moved through a four-phase development cycle.

Phase 1: The PSUSD teacher design team developed the first draft of 120 multiple choice test items and 40 constructed response tasks. These items and tasks were then distributed across four different versions of the test.

Phase 2: Editors from the Center for Performance Assessment conducted a Quality Review of each test item that included limited piloting and editing of content and assessment design.

Phase 3: The PSUSD teacher design team conducted a review of test items for bias, clarity, and relevance to the identified "Power Standards" and the district curriculum.

Phase 4: The Center for Performance Assessment produced final copies of four versions of each assessment.

Q. What are "Power Standards"?

A. Every school district in the nation has some form of local or state academic content standards. These standards describe what students are expected to know and be able to do. The standards do not, however, give the classroom teacher and school leader clarity about which standards are the most important for future success. Because of the limitations of time and the extraordinary variety in learning backgrounds of students, teachers and leaders need focus and clarity in order to prepare their students for success in high school. "Power Standards" help to provide that focus and clarity. The "Power Standards" make up what is known as the "Safety Net Curriculum."

The "Safety Net" is a very limited set of academic standards organized for each grade and for each subject. It is *not* the total curriculum – just the "safety net" that every teacher should ensure that every student knows.

The purpose of the Safety Net is to empower teachers to make wise decisions about what is most important in the curriculum. The Safety Net is not a device to ignore everything else in the curriculum, but rather a mechanism to help teachers separate the critical elements of a curriculum from learning objectives that are less important. Different teachers will make different choices, depending on the needs of their students, about what they will cover outside of the Safety Net. But every teacher should ensure that every student understands the items inside of the Safety Net. The simple truth is this: few teachers ever cover the entire textbook or the entire curriculum. Often the decision about what to cover is based on sequence – we cover the items that are listed early in the curriculum document or textbook and do not cover the items that are listed late in those documents.

The Safety Net offers a better alternative: student learning of what is most important. The focus of the Safety Net is on learning, not on mere coverage. The Safety Net acknowledges that different teachers cover different curriculum in their classroom based on different interests and varying student needs. However, every student in the district deserves an equal opportunity for learning Safety Net standards. Although teaching approaches may differ from one teacher to another, the Safety Net allows every student in the district an opportunity for learning what is most essential. From the teacher's point of view, the Safety Net rejects the approach of some states that insist on micro-management of daily lesson plans and district-imposed daily learning objectives. Rather, the Safety Net provides teachers with broad discretion on teaching and curriculum provided that the students have achieved the Safety Net objectives.

Educators apply three screens to determine if a standard is a "Power Standard." The three screens are:

1. *What endures?* In other words, what skills and knowledge will students gain that lasts from one academic year to the next? For example, the skill of constructing an informative essay is something that students need throughout their academic career. It is a skill that endures over time. The same cannot be said, for example, of the requirement that a student memorize the formula for the area of a trapezoid.

2. *What is essential for progress to the next level of instruction?* In a continuing dialog with teachers at all grade levels, we must determine what is essential for future success. For example, when 11th grade history teachers are asked what is essential for success in their classes, they rarely responded with items of historical knowledge that should have been memorized in middle school. Rather, they typically respond that students should have skills in reading and writing, knowledge of map reading, and an understanding of the difference between democracy and authoritarianism.

3. *What contributes to understanding of other standards?* The Safety Net should be comprised of "Power Standards"- that is, those standards that, once mastered, give a student the ability to use reasoning and thinking skills to learn and understand other curriculum objectives outside of the Safety Net. For

example, in a middle school mathematics class, the properties of a triangle and rectangle might be in the Safety Net, because these understandings will allow students to comprehend information about other shapes—rhombus, trapezoid, parallelogram—that are outside of the Safety Net.

(Adapted from material written by Dr. Douglas B. Reeves)

Q. Who selected the "Power Standards"?

A. Committees of teachers throughout the Palm Springs Unified School District worked during the summer of 2001 to identify the "Power Standards", create an aligned scope and sequence, and develop course descriptions. They used the three screens of endurance, success in school and preparation for the next level of learning, and leverage to reach consensus on the "Power Standards".

Q. What do these end-of-course assessments measure?

A. Each one of the assessments measures student proficiency in the "Power Standards" identified in the course description.

Q. How can these performance assessments be a comprehensive summary of the entire year's curriculum?

A. The end-of-course assessments will not cover the entire curriculum for the year. Rather, they will assess the top "Power Standards" as determined by a weighting process engaged in by this Task Force. The performance on each assessment allows a summative 'snapshot' of how the student performed on a selection of important material. It is appropriate and even suggested that students be given projects and additional assignments to assess additional objectives.

Q. How will these end-of-course assessments be scored and graded?

A. The entire end-of-course assessment is based on a 100-point scale. The points are distributed as follows:

Multiple Choice Questions Value (Worth a total of 60 possible points):

- Each multiple-choice question is worth two points. If the student answers the question correctly, s/he earns both points. If the student answers the question incorrectly, s/he loses both points. In other words, partial credit will not be given.

Constructed Response Questions Value (Worth a total of 40 possible points):

- A Score of "Exemplary" is worth eight (8) points
- A score of "Proficient" is worth six (6) points
- A score of "Progressing" is worth four (4) points
- A score of "Not Yet Meeting the Standards" is worth zero (0) points

Grading Scale:

A= 91-100
B= 81-90
C= 70-80
F= 0-69

NOTE: In this standards-based system, the grading scale does not include the letter grade of "D." If the student is progressing toward the standard(s), s/he receives a "C." A grade of "F" is given when the performance is clearly insufficient or the task is not attempted.

Q: What is the time allocation for completing the high school end-of-course assessment?

A: This assessment is divided into two parts. Students will have two (2) hours to complete the entire assessment.

GENERAL INFORMATION AND GUIDELINES
FOR USING THE END-OF-COURSE ASSESSMENTS AND THE
TWO "PRACTICE TESTS" IN YOUR CLASSROOM

The practice assessments reflect the reserved end-of-course assessments in length and format. The practice assessments are a 'mirror image' of what teachers and students can expect to find on the reserved end-of-course assessments. All of the practice assessments contain thirty multiple choice and ten constructed response items, five of which will be answered by the student. Each constructed response item has its own scoring guide. A scoring guide for the student is also provided.

Use of the end-of-course practice assessments

The goal in a standards-based system is student proficiency in the "Power Standards". The end-of-course practice assessments provide students with the opportunity to work toward proficiency and teachers the opportunity to adjust instruction and monitor learning. Inherent in the process is the need for providing students with timely and specific feedback that allows them to improve.

Suggestions for giving timely and specific feedback to students

- Determine when and how to give the student feedback. This could be through conferring one-on-one with students while the class is involved in independent seatwork. Or the teacher may choose to circulate and give feedback while students are actually completing the tasks.

- Review the criteria in the scoring guide with the student. Point out areas in the performance that need additional work. Comments to the student such as, *"Keep trying because you are almost there"* or *"I like the way you did ___, but ____ still needs work. What can you think of that would make your answer better?"* will help to motivate students.

- Encourage the student to elaborate on what he or she can do to improve the performance rather than telling the student specifically what to correct or how to do it.

- Allow the student time to make the revisions. This can be during the class time when the task was administered. Or the teacher may set aside time later in the day for revisions. Repeat the process, if necessary.

Additional suggestions for using the "Practice Assessments"

Agree at your school to use scoring guides consistently. If Mr. Jones scores Jimmy's assessment 'Exemplary' because Jimmy tried really hard, and Ms. Johnson follows the scoring guide criteria and scores Jimmy 'Proficient,' the teachers won't reach consensus on a definition of Proficient vs. Exemplary work.

Score the *performance*, not the student. Compare the student to the standards, not to other students.

Exchange assessments so that they may be scored with colleagues. Collegial scoring serves multiple functions. It guards against the temptations to compare students or to score less than fairly based on the student performing the task. It also helps build consensus, and requires no additional time because no one teacher is doing additional work.

Remember that student responses will vary. The scoring guide provides *guidelines* for what a typical answer at each level might include. However, since many times the tasks on performance assessments require more integration of student knowledge and understanding, there will be variety in student responses. Pay particular attention to whether a response addresses the questions asked in the manner indicated in the scoring guide. For example, did the response discuss the topic or something different? Did the response contain the level of accuracy or detail required by the scoring guide?

Frequently, there is not a single "right way" to come to a correct answer. For that matter, often there is not a single 'right answer' to the tasks on the assessments. The scoring guides that accompany each task provide criteria for a score of Exemplary, Proficient, Progressing, or Not Yet Meeting the Standard.

When revising takes place, allow multiple tries until the standard is met. It is okay to repeat the tasks. Remember that you are measuring achievement, not time. It doesn't matter if the student is proficient the first time or the second time he or she attempts the task.

Make assessments and scoring guides accessible to students. *Assessments are open, not secret*. Students can and should see the entire assessment before they begin work. Knowing what lays ahead helps to focus learning. If students have access and time to work on the pre-assessments, there should be no surprises when the year-end assessments are given.

Review the scoring guides with students before beginning work. The scoring guide helps students know specifically what is expected of them. It gives feedback even before they begin. For non-reading students, read the scoring guides to them and allow them to check off the criteria they meet. Scoring guides may be posted in the classroom.

THE FORMAT OF THE ASSESSMENTS

The Palm Springs Unified School District End-of-Course Assessment Program has the following components:

- This *Educator's Guide to the Palm Springs Unified School District End-of-Course Assessments*, which should be read prior to giving the assessment.

- Four separate assessments: Two (versions A and B) to be used as practice tests during the duration of the course and two more (version C and D) to be administered alternately as the actual end-of-course assessment. Each assessment has two parts: thirty multiple choice and ten constructed response questions, five of which will be answered by the student.

- Directions for administration of the assessments.

- Answer keys for the multiple-choice portion of the assessment.

- The scoring guides (rubrics) and answer keys for the constructed response portion of the assessments.

SCORING GUIDES

- A score of *"Proficient"* means that the student has clearly met the objective(s) contained in the scoring guide criteria. However, a score of "Proficient" should not be given to a student if the response contains additional information that is incorrect or irrelevant.

- A score of *"Exemplary"* should be given only for student responses that include correct or relevant elements that are beyond or in addition to the required elements of proficiency. This level of performance illustrates additional application or synthesis of knowledge. An "Exemplary" response does not merely contain three examples if the scoring guide asked only asked for two examples. Rather, an exemplary response contains advanced innovation, sophistication, or additional insights or connections.

- A *"Progressing"* response must contain some, but not all of the elements of a correct response as outlined in the "Proficient" score. It is difficult to outline all of the possible combinations for student responses. Therefore, a "Progressing" score should be applied to student responses that do not meet all of the criteria for "Proficient."

- *"Not Yet Meeting the Standards"* is given to a response that clearly indicates the student does not understand the questions, does not have mastery of the material, or the task is not complete enough to be evaluated.

SCORING THE ASSESSMENTS

As the teacher scores a student's response to a task, it is important to remember that *the performance is compared to standards, not to other students*. The number of students who receive a score at any of the performance levels may vary tremendously.

Each task on the constructed response portion of the assessment contains a specific scoring guide that the teacher will use to determine the performance of students. Students also receive a scoring guide that identifies what it is they must do to demonstrate proficiency. The scoring guide for students is a way for students to self-evaluate.

ACCOMMODATIONS FOR
ESL, 504, AND SPECIAL EDUCATION STUDENTS

Students with disabilities shall take the end-of-course assessment with those accommodations that are consistent with their Individualized Education Program or their section 504 Plan provided that the accommodations do not fundamentally alter what the test measures.

English Language Learners (ELL's) are also required to take the end-of-course assessments. ELL students who are functioning in a class where English is spoken will receive no special accommodation.

The following accommodations are not allowed because they have been determined to fundamentally alter what the test measures.

- Calculators on the math portion of the end-of-course assessments.
- Audio or oral presentation of the English/Language Arts portion of the test.

CONTACT INFORMATION

In Palm Springs Unified School District:

- Your site test coordinator will be able to provide you with information about the administration and use of the practice and reserved end-of-course assessments.
- Mr. Frank Tinney, Director of Standards, Assessment and Accountability, 760-416-6079

From the Center for Performance Assessment:

We welcome your thoughts, ideas, and suggestions about your experience with using the assessment materials. We also know that using performance assessments in the classroom is a sophisticated act of teaching. We offer assistance for your assessment questions.

- www.makingstandardswork.com
- (800) 844-6599

Frequently Asked Questions

Within the context of the first six chapters, many of the questions educators ask as they identify their Power Standards have been addressed. The purpose of Chapter Seven is to provide an additional resource of specific questions and responses to assist educators as they implement the ideas presented in this book within their own school systems.

The following questions and responses have been selected from thousands of e-mails received by the Center for Performance Assessment. The casual and conversational tone of these exchanges is deliberately informal. Readers who wish a more formal examination of the issues concerning Power Standards may wish to consult Dr. Douglas B. Reeves' *Accountability in Action* (2000) and *Leader's Guide to Standards* (2002).

The questions are presented in no particular order. Dr. Reeves has generously contributed many of the responses, and I have indicated which responses are his by including his initials parenthetically at the end of the response.

Q: How long does the process of identifying the Power Standards take, and when do busy educators ever find time to do this?

A: The issue of "never having enough time" is, in fact, the very reason for identifying Power Standards in the first place. If people see the time issue as a barrier to accomplishing this important work, they first need to understand that the time they invest in the development and articulation of Power Standards *saves time* in the long run because educators will have *more* instructional time to teach the standards and indicators that matter the most for depth of understanding.

It takes surprisingly less time to identify Power Standards than people initially think. Many districts have accomplished the identification of Power Standards within one content area, including the review and feedback by all educators, in as little as a month or two, depending on the size of the district. Once everyone is familiar with the process, it can be repeated in other content areas of choice. However, it is not unusual for Power Standards in several content areas to be identified simultaneously. Finding the time is always an issue. Rather than trying to find and schedule an entire day to work through the initial process, some school faculties I have worked with have allocated time during their weekly or monthly staff meetings, grade-level meetings, or department meetings to identify their Power Standards. Over the course of several meetings, the work has been concluded in relatively little time.

We all know that when something important needs to be done, people will find the time to get it accomplished. It all depends on priorities, organization, and focus.

Q: Is there a "standard" national set of Power Standards?

A: There is no such thing as a "standard" national set of Power Standards. Each district should develop its own Power Standards with teacher participation at the building level. If each building engaged in a process of Power Standards selection and the district accumulated that information, they would see a great deal of commonality among the teachers and then be able to say, "This is not something the district is unilaterally mandating, but reflects the collective wisdom of all our teachers." In other words, we teach the process and provide examples, but we will not simply tell them what their Power Standards should be. (DR)

Q: How many Power Standards should there be for each grade or content area? I noticed that Wayne Township in Indiana identified very few indicators and other school systems have identified many. Is there a fractional formula that we can follow?

A: I suggest narrowing the standards within one content area for a particular grade to approximately one-third of the total number. There is no hard and fast rule to this, but on average, this seems to be about right. Read on, however, to gain Dr. Reeves' perspective on this issue:

Power Standards are a subset of the entire list of state academic content standards, not a repetition of them. When someone recently told me that his district had narrowed their original list of more than 80 standards down to 44 Power Standards, he was quite pleased. Although this is a good start, such a conservative reduction is not sufficient for the focus that teachers and students need. My rule of thumb is 7 to 12 Power Standards per subject per grade. If you have more than that, then you can't possibly assess them every month or every quarter, as you should. If you are only checking a standard once a year for proficiency, this standard cannot be a Power Standard. Moreover, any identified Power Standard (writing, charts/graphs, reading skill and comprehension) is so important, students need to see it represented in many different subjects, not just one. (DR)

Q: What do I do about the standards that are not identified as Power Standards?

A: Power Standards don't exclude teaching other standards that are not so designated; they do, however, give me a clear set of priorities. When I'm short on time, I know that it's more important to triple my time on a Power Standard so that every student becomes proficient and that my already proficient students become exemplary, than to superficially "expose" students to every standard on my list. (DR)

Q: If I emphasize only the Power Standards, won't I be neglecting to teach my students concepts and skills from other standards that are sure to be on the state test?

A: This is by far the biggest bone of contention among teachers, curriculum directors, and assessment people when the subject of Power Standards arises. Some standards are unequivocally more important than others, period. What you will find is that a good set of Power Standards will cover about 88% of the items on the state test, but not

100%. If you go after that extra 12%, you will have to cover many more standards and hence have less teaching time to thoroughly teach each of the Power Standards. The rationale for deeply teaching the Power Standards is simply this: it is wiser to have students proficient at 88% of what will likely be on the test rather than have them exposed to 100% of what *could* be on the test, but proficient at only a few of those items. (DR)

Q: How can we use the annual state test to inform our selection of Power Standards when the test changes yearly or we are told to teach everything "to be safe"?

A: Dr. Reeves' response to the question above relates also to this question. State assessments *predominantly* test important knowledge and skills, not obscure facts and details. Use your test data and your state's Test Information Guide to inform your decision-making process. Remember that identifying Power Standards with the collective insights and experience of veteran teachers will narrow the gap of uncertainty as to what is likely to be on the test, even if the test changes. Teaching those Power Standards for depth of understanding will do the most to prepare students for success, not only on the state test, but in school and life as well.

Q: How can we reach consensus about which standards should be included, especially when involving so many people—all with such strong opinions?

A: Dr. Reeves has answered this one better than anyone. "Forget the myth of trying to get 100% buy-in. Go for a super-majority consensus, which means approximately 80% of the participants agree. With a simple majority, nearly half the group is disenfranchised. If you can reach a super-majority percentage, you have a substantial consensus."

Q: What if our individual school thinks we need different Power Standards than the district's version? Our student learning needs and our own test data indicate that in a couple of areas, we need to emphasize standards that are not the district Power Standards.

A: The purpose of having district-wide Power Standards is for equity and consistency throughout the district. If students move from one school to another school within the district, the Power Standards will still be the same. District-wide Power Standards also provide a common focus. The curriculum, teaching expertise, instructional methods, lessons and activities, and teacher-created assessments organized around a common set of Power Standards can be shared among educators within a district.

Schools whose test data, student learning needs, and School Improvement Plans indicate that particular standards and indicators other than the district Power Standards must be emphasized in order to see improvements specific to their needs ought to have the freedom to do so. This does not mean that they are given license to disregard the district Power Standards. But they should be able to emphasize other standards and indicators *along with* the district's Power Standards in order to realize better results within their own student population.

If a district has identified Power Standards that truly meet the criteria of leverage, endurance, and preparation for the next level of learning—including successful performance on the state tests—an individual school may find it unnecessary to emphasize any others.

Q: My faculty is resisting the requirement that we use standards, claiming that it is an infringement of their academic freedom. What can I say in response to this?

A: The issue here is about the effective implementation of *standards*, not standardization, which implies that everyone must teach the same standards in the same way. By focusing on a set of prioritized standards that represent essential student learning outcomes, educators can draw upon their own individual talents, insights, expertise, and creativity to help their students deeply grasp the concepts and skills they need to know.

Q: You talk about resistance from faculty. What about resistance from parents, administrators, and state department officials?

A: The issue of most concern to these stakeholders is performance. If students perform better academically, parents will be happy. The best examples in this regard are Advanced Placement classes in the most competitive high schools. Parents often think of the AP exam as the metaphor for their child's aptitude. Students do not memorize every item on the AP test, but focus instead on the critical skills, reasoning, and thinking abilities that will help them improve on test performance.

With regard to resistance from administrators and state department officials, I would ask this question: What do administrators and state department officials emphasize most, coverage of everything in the textbook or academic performance as measured on state tests? If the answer is the latter—and I know of nowhere in the country where this is not the case—then the issue is *results*. If a school were to use Power Standards or any other technique and fail to improve student performance, then administrators and state department officials would be unhappy. If a school uses Power Standards and student performance improves, then administrators and state department officials are delighted. Therefore, the only question is this: Do Power Standards improve academic performance? In fact, we have already developed case studies around the nation that prove the obvious: *Focusing on key academic standards is effective.* But no one at the Center for Performance Assessment has ever asserted that Power Standards alone are the cause of improved student achievement. This is but one technique among many that is necessary for improved achievement. Schools that only focus on Power Standards, but fail to reallocate the way that they spend time, fail to collaboratively score student work, and fail to dramatically increase nonfiction writing with editing and rewriting should not expect much improvement.

What Power Standards do is to allow the classroom teacher to focus. Focus dispels the illusion that frantic coverage is equivalent to student learning. Focus must include time for more literacy instruction, time for more student feedback, and time for more teacher collaboration. Schools that implement a carefully selected, manageable number of key practices to improve academic achievement, and then monitor that implementation every week at the classroom level, will see improved results. (DR)

Q: How can the identification of Power Standards assist educators who work with special education students and English language learners?

A: Rather than face the daunting task of imparting *all* of the academic content standards to students with special learning needs and/or limited English proficiency, educators can instead focus their efforts on making sure these students learn the Power Standards. Since these prioritized standards represent the "essential" knowledge and skills all students need, educators will be spending their valuable instructional time helping them learn the standards that are the most important. These students will thus be better prepared to succeed in school each year, in life, and on the state assessments that they are required to take.

When writing IEPs (Individualized Education Plans), special education teachers can utilize the Power Standards to help determine specific learning goals for their students. Since these educators daily serve students in several different grade levels, Power Standards enable them to quickly focus on the grade-specific, prioritized standards that are critical for their students to learn and then modify instruction and assessment according to individual student needs.

Power Standards can be especially helpful to educators working with a student population comprised of diverse primary language backgrounds. Educators who instruct English language learners can better utilize second-language acquisition techniques to impart the *most important* standards to students instead of trying, with varying degrees of success, to teach *all* of the standards.

Q: What is the role of the school leader(s) in the Power Standards identification process?

A: The school administrator plays a vital role in the successful implementation of this practice. S/he first needs to thoroughly understand the process and then help the faculty identify the Power Standards. This can best be accomplished by making it possible for teachers to meet together and collaborate. Collectively, most faculties possess the expertise needed to identify the Power Standards. But it is usually the administrator who serves as a catalyst for getting the work started and completed. This means scheduling the time for teachers to meet in groups (grade-level or department), establishing norms for productive collaboration, and then providing whatever support is needed for them to accomplish the work. Such support may include materials, personnel, physical space, incentives or stipends for work done outside of the contracted work day, etc. The administrator is the coach, the cheerleader, and the quarterback in leading his or her team to a victory in this regard.

Q: Why doesn't our state department of education just give us the state standards in this type of prioritized format? Why are we left to do this on our own?

A: Just as the individual 50 states have not adopted a national set of academic content standards and have preferred instead to decide what their own standards should be, local districts need to decide for themselves which of the state standards are the most important for their students to learn.

Were the states to prioritize the standards, many educators would greatly appreciate knowing the state perspective on which standards "mattered the most." Certain states are beginning to do this. California, for example, has identified the "key standards" in each of the strands of mathematics and notated those standards as being the most important ones to be covered within a grade level. As a general rule, however, states have endeavored to determine everything that they believe students should know and be able to do by the time they leave high school and then left the implementation of this blueprint to the local districts.

Q: Our standards in certain content areas are still in revision form at the state level. Should we delay the identification of Power Standards until the final versions are published?

A: Obviously, if the final drafts are due to be published soon, it makes sense to wait rather than to do all the Power Standards identification work twice. If this is not the case, it makes more sense to begin the process with the current standards drafts you have and then make needed revisions once the final documents are published. Making revisions to your draft version of Power Standards would certainly be easier than having to start from the beginning once the new drafts of the standards are published.

Even more importantly, teaching and learning cannot wait. If educators can reference even a first draft of Power Standards while planning instruction and assessment, their students will be further ahead than if they continue to use the coverage model of instruction while waiting for the final drafts to be completed.

Q: How often should our Power Standards be revised?

A: Certainly when key variables change, you should revise the Power Standards. These variables include changes in the state test or crucial decisions that have been made which will affect instruction or assessment. I would bet that 80% or more of the Power Standards will remain in place, but it will build confidence in any process if every two to three years you conduct a review—admit mistakes, make improvements, and get more buy-in from stakeholders. (DR)

Q: Is there any additional advice you would offer groups as they look for vertical alignment of the Power Standards between the grades and grade spans?

A: Yes. Have each group include a teacher at the next higher grade. It's not the same when fifth grade teachers look at the sixth grade standards as when fifth grade teachers are going through the standards for the next grade and hear a sixth grade teacher say, "Look, you don't need to devote energy to polyhedrons. What I really need you to do is to invest instructional time reviewing with your students what they should have learned in fourth grade math and then teach the fifth grade math Power Standards thoroughly so that by the time they come to me, they are totally proficient with number operations and ready for the sixth grade math Power Standards." This lends tremendous credibility toward ensuring true vertical alignment. (DR and LA)

You might also consider including in the Power Standards discussions how other faculty members from different disciplines fit into the picture. For example, a good Power Standards-related discussion might include how the music and art teachers can plan some of their instruction and activities to help students develop specific competencies in fractions or other content area Power Standards. (DR)

Conclusion

Readers who have additional questions regarding Power Standards are encouraged to contact the Center for Performance Assessment. Questions will be forwarded to our staff of educational consultants who will be more than happy to reply.

Center for Performance Assessment
800-844-6599
www.MakingStandardsWork.com

CHAPTER EIGHT

Identifying Power Standards: The Step-by-Step Process

The purpose of this chapter is to provide a summary of the steps any school system can follow to accomplish the identification of their Power Standards. My intent is to present this series of steps, repeated from preceding chapters without the explanatory commentary, in a checklist format for easy reference by educators working through the Power Standards process.

Power Standards Identification Process

← Present rationale for Power Standards

← Agree on definition of terms (standards, indicators, benchmarks, etc.)

← Pose guiding question:

"What knowledge and skills do this year's students need so they will enter next year's class with confidence and a readiness for success?"

← Determine criteria for Power Standards selection:

- Endurance

- Leverage

- Readiness for next level of learning

- What students need for success in school, in life, on state tests

← Define role of participants:

- Develop first drafts of Power Standards in grade span groups

- Plan how to share drafts and receive feedback at sites

- Revise drafts based on feedback received

- Assist in implementation of Power Standards at sites

← Begin Power Standards identification process:

- Select a content area

- Divide participants into grade-span groups

- Select particular section within content area in which to begin

- Begin process in ONE grade within the grade span
- Review agreed-upon selection criteria
- Individuals mark Power Standards choices ALONE
- Compare selections with colleagues
- Note similarities and differences; reach preliminary consensus
- Consult state's Testing Information Guide and district test data
- Revise selected Power Standards to reflect what will be tested
- Record selections on large pieces of chart paper, one chart per grade
- Repeat process for grade below and grade above
- Grade spans post their charts in K-12 progression
- Look for vertical alignment *within* grade span
- Identify gaps, overlaps, and omissions
- Revise selections as needed on charts
- Look for gaps, overlaps, omissions *between* grade spans
- Revise selections as needed
- Sequence Power Standards by reporting periods (optional)

← Develop action plan for sharing drafts and receiving feedback at sites:

- Share information with building principals
- Schedule faculty meetings to present information
- Develop a plan and schedule for grade levels and departments to create their own Power Standards drafts
- Review drafts from district meeting; compare/contrast/revise
- Gather revised drafts or feedback from each site
- Schedule district meeting to review feedback from all sites
- Do second revision of drafts based on feedback
- Send back to sites for final review (optional)
- Publish and distribute final versions of Power Standards to sites
- See also 11-step agenda for district meeting(s) in Chapter 3

← Plan related follow-up activities:

- Develop instructional guides or curriculum frameworks to implement Power Standards
- Develop end-of-course and grade-level assessments aligned to Power Standards
- Revise reporting system to reflect Power Standards

This is by no means an all-inclusive checklist of all the activities a school system may engage in to identify and implement Power Standards. Each school and district will recognize the need to make many changes in curriculum, instructional practices, assessment, and reporting of student progress as a direct result of their establishment of Power Standards. But these changes will, over time, inevitably lead to the goal of all educational restructuring—that of increased student success in school, improved student performance on all assessment measures, and a more effective preparation of students for adult life.

When educators express concern as to how long it will take them to identify all their Power Standards and then implement an assessment system aligned to them, I offer a bit of logic to encourage them. Even if it does take several months or even a year or more to identify all the Power Standards and get them fully implemented throughout the district, what does it matter? That time will pass anyway! The difference is, when the work is finished, you will have a *district-owned process and product* that everyone can use to improve instruction and assessment. Time well spent indeed!

It may be helpful to share with everyone the following slogan when the Power Standards identification work begins: it is a *process*, not an event; a *marathon*, not a sprint!

CHAPTER NINE

"Unwrapping" Power Standards

From Power Standards to "Unwrapping"

The identification of Power Standards is often the first step school systems take in effectively implementing standards. Once this is accomplished, attention turns to aligning the Power Standards with curriculum, instruction, and assessment. One of the most powerful practices for imparting the Power Standards to students is called "unwrapping" the standards.

"Unwrapping" the standards and indicators is a simple process for making standards *manageable*. I developed it in collaboration with others across the country to help educators extract from the wording of the standards the concepts and skills students need to know and be able to do. These "unwrapped" concepts and skills are represented on a graphic organizer and then used to plan lessons, focus instruction, and drive assessment.

Educators next identify the "Big Ideas," or lasting understandings, from the "unwrapped" concepts and skills that they want students to discover on their own and remember long after instruction ends. With these Big Ideas clearly in mind, they then formulate "Essential Questions" to share with students at the inception of an instructional unit. These questions guide educators in the selection of lessons and activities they will use to advance student understanding of the "unwrapped" concepts and skills. The goal is for students to be able to answer the Essential Questions with the Big Ideas *stated in their own words* by the conclusion of an instructional unit.

Often educators who have completed the Power Standards identification process and later learn about "unwrapping" the standards remark, "We wish we had had the 'unwrapping' information *first*. It would have made it much easier to prioritize the standards by importance since the key concepts and skills contained within them would have been more readily apparent."

One process may indeed inform the other, but regardless of which one is experienced first, the two together make a powerful combination for improving instruction and learning. The "unwrapping" standards process can be successfully applied not only to those standards that have been systematically identified as "power," but also to *all* standards in every grade and in every content area.

The full explanation of the rationale and process for "unwrapping" the standards can be found in the *Power Standards* companion volume, *"Unwrapping" The Standards* (Ainsworth, 2003). It offers an in-depth explanation of how to determine Big Ideas, write Essential Questions, and "work smarter, not harder" by involving *all* educators in a particular school and/or district in the "unwrapping" standards process. Owing to the contributions of K-12 educators across the country who generously shared their work for the publication of this book, there are over 80 examples of "unwrapped" standards from a variety of different content areas.

From "Unwrapping" Standards to Performance Assessment

In the Center for Performance Assessment's professional development seminar, *Making Standards Work*, named after Dr. Douglas B. Reeves' pioneering book by the same title (1996), educators work collaboratively to design a standards-based performance assessment. The design steps of Dr. Reeves' performance assessment model include:

1. Target "essential" standards and indicators within one content area.

2. Make interdisciplinary connections by identifying related standards and indicators in *other* content areas.

3. Create an Engaging Scenario to "hook" student interest.

4. Design a collection of several related performance tasks that enable students to develop their understanding of the targeted standards.

5. Write task-specific scoring guides or rubrics to evaluate the degree of proficiency in the work that students produce.

I expanded the five steps above to include the "unwrapping" of the targeted standards, the identification of Big Ideas, and the writing of Essential Questions and then rearranged the sequence of design steps so that the model now looks like this:

1. Target "essential" (Power) standards and indicators in one content area.

2. "Unwrap" those standards and indicators; create graphic organizer.

3. Identify the Big Ideas.

4. Write the Essential Questions.

5. Design the performance assessment tasks to guide instruction and assessment.

6. Identify interdisciplinary standards and indicators reflected in tasks.

7. Create an Engaging Scenario to introduce and link performance tasks.

8. Develop scoring guides or rubrics to assess the performance tasks.

Typically, the seminar is conducted over three days. On the first day, participants complete steps one through four. On the second day, they complete steps five through seven. And on the final day, they complete step eight and leave the seminar with a first draft, "unwrapped" standards-based performance assessment ready to use in their own instructional programs.

Individual schools and entire school systems have a limited number of hours and days available each year for professional development. If three *consecutive* days are not available to complete all the components of the performance assessment model, participants begin with the one-day workshop on "unwrapping." They can implement that part of the process in their own programs and then return days, weeks, or even months later to complete the remaining components of the performance assessment model.

Foundation First

Identifying Power Standards and then "unwrapping" them are the first critical steps to effectively managing the standards. Even if educators have not yet designed performance assessment tasks guided by the Essential Questions as a way to systematically develop student understanding of the "unwrapped" concepts, skills, and Big Ideas, they can utilize their own teaching talents and expertise to help students grasp the Big Ideas and answer the Essential Questions. They can design their own assessments that will reflect what they want their students to learn. The improvements they witness in student achievement will motivate them to say, "This really worked! What else can I do?" And that is where they can consider designing an "unwrapped," standards-based performance assessment as the next logical step.

How Powerful Practices Work Together

Over time, powerful practices can produce significant changes in the quality of instruction and the achievement of all students. As with any new change, we need to remember to introduce new ideas *one at a time* and then build consensus for their effectiveness *through results* before introducing the next new idea. Start with the identification of Power Standards and implement them effectively with participation by all stakeholders. Once that practice is underway, introduce "unwrapping" the standards. When everyone is experiencing success with "unwrapping," there will be greater receptivity to developing performance assessments aligned to the "unwrapped" Power Standards.

At the conclusion of a three-day *Making Standards Work* seminar held in Montgomery County, Ohio, in the spring of 2002, Mark Jones, a middle school educator from the school district of New Lebanon, greeted me enthusiastically. It was the first time I had seen Mark since the previous fall when I had shared the Power Standards and "unwrapping" the standards information with the New Lebanon Middle School faculty and principal, Susan E. Riegle.

"Larry, we just received the results of our Ohio Sixth Grade Proficiency Test. We're pretty excited since we made some big improvements."

As Mark was about to show me the Disaggregate Analysis report from the state, Ed Mathes joined us. Ed is with the Montgomery County Educational Service Center and serves as the Curriculum Supervisor for New Lebanon Schools.

Ed said to me, "Do you remember when you shared with us your circle graphic of how powerful practices work together to improve student achievement? Once we saw that, we knew we had found our game plan."

Ed was referring to a diagram that I created which lists the following practices around the circumference of a circle: Data-Driven Decision Making, Power Standards, "Unwrapping" the Standards, Big Ideas, Essential Questions, Effective Teaching Strategies, Performance Assessments, and Scoring Guides (Rubrics). I had explained during my visit to New Lebanon that a school or district could begin with any one of the practices on the circle. After each of these practices had been systematically implemented over time, the resulting improvements in student learning would indeed be significant.

Ed went on to say, "Under Susie Riegle's direction, we decided to focus first on the identification of our Power Standards. After you showed us how to 'unwrap' the standards on your second visit to New Lebanon, we began that practice. All of our middle school teachers really began to emphasize writing in their instructional programs. We began using performance tasks and assessing student work with scoring guides."

I said, "Don't keep me in suspense! Let's see these results!"

Mark handed me the test score report and said, "This table compares the percentage of New Lebanon sixth graders who passed the Ohio Proficiency Test in the 2000-01 school year with those who did so in the 2001-02 school year.

Total Group	Writing	Reading	Math	Citizenship	Science
2001-2002	93%	58%	70%	81%	68%
2000-2001	78.3%	44.3%	63.2%	60.4%	58.5%

Mark continued, "Although these are different classes of sixth grade students taking the test, our demographics did not change. Our faculty members did not change. The only variable that we are certain *did* change, is that we all started implementing the powerful practices on your circle graphic. And we did this in less than a year!"

After congratulating them on their success, I added, "These commendable results are only the beginning! As all of you continue to refine these practices, think of the additional gains you will make in the coming years!"

Such testimonials from real educators in real school systems provide the evidence that these practices are not merely theories—they work!

Contact Information

If you have any questions as you work through the Power Standards process, please do not hesitate to contact my colleagues or me at the Center for Performance Assessment. We are happy to assist you in whatever ways we can. Our contact information is listed below.

Best wishes as you continue to strive to achieve educational excellence for all the students you serve!

Larry Ainsworth, M.S.
Executive Director of Professional Development
Center for Performance Assessment
800-844-6599, ext. 509
www.MakingStandardsWork.com

"The 'Safety Net' Curriculum" by Douglas B. Reeves, Ph.D.

What is the Safety Net Curriculum?

The Safety Net is a very limited set of learning objectives organized for each grade and for each subject. It is *not* the total curriculum – just the "safety net" that every teacher should ensure that every student knows.

What Is the Purpose of the Safety Net Curriculum?

The purpose of the Safety Net is to empower teachers to make wise decisions about what is most important in the curriculum. The Safety Net is not a device to ignore everything else in the curriculum, but rather a mechanism to help teachers separate the critical elements of a curriculum from learning objectives that are less important. Different teachers will make different choices, depending on the needs of their students, about what they will cover outside of the Safety Net. But every teacher should ensure that every student understands the items inside of the Safety Net. The simple truth is this: few teachers ever cover the entire textbook or the entire curriculum. Often the decision about what to cover is based on sequence – we cover the items that are listed early in the curriculum document or textbook, and so we do not cover the items that are listed late in those documents. The Safety Net offers a better alternative: student learning of what is most important. The focus of the Safety Net is on learning, not on mere coverage. The Safety Net acknowledges that different teachers cover different curriculum in their classroom based on different interests and varying student needs. However, every student in the district deserves an equal opportunity for learning Safety Net standards. However different teaching approaches may be from one teacher to another, the Safety Net allows every student in the district an opportunity for learning what is most essential. From the teacher's point of view, the Safety Net rejects the approach of some states that insist on micro-management of daily lesson plans and district-imposed daily learning objectives. Rather, the Safety Net provides teachers with broad discretion on teaching and curriculum *provided that the students have achieved the Safety Net objectives.*

What's Wrong with the Standards and Curriculum We Already Have?

Many teachers and administrators have complained that traditional standards, curricula, and textbooks are too voluminous to have practical value. Some analysts, such as Robert Marzano of the Mid-continent Research for Education and Learning (McREL), have concluded that most states would require school years almost *double* their present length in order to adequately cover existing standards. The Safety Net provides focus so those teachers can have a common understanding of what is necessary for all students. The Safety Net specifically provides an emphasis on student learning of a few objectives rather than student exposure to many objectives.

How Did You Choose the Learning Objectives in the Safety Net?

Three questions guide the selection of Safety Net learning objectives:

1. **What endures?** In other words, what skills and knowledge will students gain that last from one academic year to the next? For example, the skill of constructing an informative essay is something that students need throughout their academic career. It is a skill that endures over time. The same cannot be said, for example, of the requirement that a student memorize the formula for the area of a trapezoid.

2. **What is essential for progress to the next level of instruction?** In a continuing dialog with teachers at all grade levels, we much determine what is essential for future success. For example, when 11th grade history teachers are asked what is essential for success in their classes, they rarely respond with items of historical knowledge that should have been memorized in middle school. Rather, they typically respond that students should have skills in reading and writing, knowledge of map reading, and an understanding of the difference between democracy and authoritarianism.

3. **What contributes to understanding of other standards?** The Safety Net should comprise "power standards"—that is, those standards that, once mastered, give a student the ability to use reasoning and thinking skills to learn and understand other curriculum objectives outside of the Safety Net. For example, in a middle school mathematics class, the properties of a triangle and rectangle might be in the Safety Net, because this understanding will allow students to comprehend information about other shapes—rhombus, trapezoid, parallelogram – that are outside of the Safety Net.

If Students Know the Safety Net Objectives, Can We Ignore All the Other Standards?

No. The state standards and district curriculum remain important guides for teachers in planning their instruction. However, few if any teachers will actually cover every element of every portion of state standards and district curriculum. To the extent that a teacher, by virtue of a careful analysis of the needs of students, covers less than the entire curriculum and state standards, the Safety Net provides a guide for the essential core curriculum that must not only be covered, but that the students must learn.

Power Standards for the Middle Grades by Douglas B. Reeves, Ph.D.

The Need for Power Standards

Every school district in the nation has some form of local or state academic content standards. These standards describe what students are expected to know and be able to do. The standards do not, however, give the classroom teacher and school leader clarity about which standards are the most important for future success. Because of the limitations of time and the extraordinary variety in learning backgrounds of middle school students, teachers and leaders need focus and clarity in order to prepare their students for success in high school. Power Standards help to provide that focus and clarity.

Grades Are Not Enough: Students Must Be Proficient

In a recent study of middle schools conducted by the Center for Performance Assessment, the difference in average grade-point average for those students attending high-achieving middle schools was one-tenth of one point higher than the GPA for those students attending very low-achieving middle schools. In other words, grades typically do not tell students if they are adequately prepared for high school. By contrast, the requirement that students demonstrate proficiency of a few "power standards" is a clear and consistent mandate for high expectations and adequate preparation.

Making Time the Variable

In a traditional middle school setting, students in a 7th grade classroom may have reading levels ranging from 3rd grade to 12th grade. The assumption that all of these students will become proficient in the same amount of time with the same amount of teaching is absurd. In the typical uniform curriculum and standard schedule, these students will leave middle school with the same widely varying abilities with which they entered. Unfortunately, this means that many of these students will enter high school woefully unprepared for the challenges they will face. The clear and simple truth is this: some students need more time to become proficient. Placing all students in the same schedule and expecting uniform results is a prescription for failure. Some students need more time for literacy and math. Denying them this extra time is as harmful as denying unvaccinated students the appropriate medical treatment because "they should have had the vaccinations before they got to middle school."

What About the Other Parts of the Curriculum?

The Power Standards are definitely not exhaustive. They represent the "core of the core" – the essential knowledge and skills students must have to enter high school. If they do not have these skills at the beginning of 8th grade, teachers and school leaders should ensure that the students receive the schedule, curriculum, coaching, and intervention necessary to ensure proficiency in these Power Standards.

The Power Standards:
What Middle School Students Need to
Enter High School with Confidence and Success

Writing, Reading, and Social Studies:

Students will use Standard English, including proper grammar, spelling, and punctuation, to complete the following independently evaluated essays. Teachers will evaluate the essays using the same district-wide writing rubric that is routinely used in the classroom for all writing assignments.

- *Narrative*: Given a new short story of approximately 1,500 words, students will write a five-paragraph essay describing the setting, characters, and plot.

- *Analytical*: Write a five-paragraph essay comparing the points of view expressed in two authentic historical documents.

- *Persuasive*: Write a letter to the editor of a local newspaper expressing a point of view on a topic of interest. Include evidence to support your point of view.

Mathematics and Science:

- Perform number operations (addition, subtraction, multiplication, and division) from ten-thousandths to millions with and without a calculator.

- Given a story problem presented in narrative form, draw a picture that describes the problem and write word and number sentences that describe the steps to the solution.

- Draw an accurate two-dimensional scale drawing of a real world object. Include a demonstration of an understanding of the properties of rectangles and triangles, complete linear and area measurements, and accurate use of scale.

- Given a scientific question, generate a hypothesis, design an experiment, conduct measurements of at least two variables, place the data in a table, create an appropriate graph from the data in the table, and write a paragraph that correctly states the conclusions to be drawn from the experiment.

Teamwork, Organization, and Service:

- Participate in a team in which each student shares responsibility for planning, organization, and execution of an original idea with value to fellow students and school community. Submit the project to evaluation by teachers and other adults.

References

Ainsworth, L. and Christinson, J. (2000). *Five easy steps to a balanced math program.* Denver: Advanced Learning Press.

Ainsworth, L. (2003). *"Unwrapping" the standards: A simple process to make standards <u>manageable</u>.* Denver: Advanced Learning Press.

Jacobs, H. H. (1997). *Mapping the big picture: Integrating curriculum and assessment K-12.* Alexandria, VA: ASCD.

Olson, L. (2002). "States anxious for federal guidance on yearly progress." *Education Week,* November 27, 2002, p. 15.

Reeves, D. B. (2000). *Accountability in action: A blueprint for learning organizations.* Denver: Advanced Learning Press.

Reeves, D. B. (2002). *The leader's guide to standards: A blueprint for educational equity and excellence.* San Francisco: Jossey-Bass.

Reeves, D. B. (1996) *Making standards work.* Denver: Advanced Learning Press.

Sherer, M. "How and why standards can improve student achievement: A conversation with Robert J. Marzano." *Education Leadership,* September, 2001, pp. 14-18.

Wiggins, G., and McTighe, J. (2000). *Understanding by design.* Upper Saddle River, NJ: Prentice Hall.

Index

Notes

Notes